Raising Pure Teens

10 Strategies to Protect (or Restore) Your Teenager's Innocence

Jason Evert and
Chris Stefanick

Totus Tuus
— P R E S S —
Denver
2013

Raising Pure Teens
Jason Evert and Chris Stefanick
©2013, Totus Tuus Press, LLC.
Sixth Edition

Published by Totus Tuus Press, LLC.
PO Box 280021
Lakewood, CO 80228
www.totustuuspress.com

Cover by Devin Schadt
Interior design by Russell Design

Printed in the United States of America
ISBN 978-0-9894905-5-9

TABLE OF CONTENTS

Introduction 1

Strategies to Win the Battle:

1. *Pray!* 19

2. *Understand their motives.* 39

3. *Teach your teen to say "YES."* 59

4. *Be a parent first and not a buddy.* 69

5. *Beware of sex education.* 85

6. *Set the standard high and clear.* 101

7. *Protect your teen from the media.* 115

8. *Delay the onset of dating.* 129

9. *Have THE talk (but make sure it's part of a lifetime of talks)* 147

10. *Model chastity in marriage.* 171

Conclusion 187

Resources 191

Endnotes 205

TABLE OF CONTENTS

Introduction ....

Strategies to Win the Battle

1. The Beginning ....

2. Discovering the ....

3. Your Questions and Your ....

4. Discover What ....

5. Develop a Foundation 85

6. Develop a Battle Plan, Step by 101

7. Write Your Vision 115

8. Discover the ....

9. Build a Team of Inner Circle ....

10. Stay on Track ....

11. Building the Right ....

Conclusion ....

Resources 191

References 205

INTRODUCTION

A teenage girl in Florida sent and received a total of 35,463 text messages in a single month according to the Associated Press.[1] That's 1,182 a day, or nearly one per minute, if you're counting. Although she had tallied more than 30,000 monthly messages before, she attributed the most recent spike to the fact that she needed to keep in touch with friends during cheerleading camp.

How is a parent to keep up? It's easy to feel overwhelmed by a teen's fast-paced life. But monitoring a thousand texts per day is the least of our worries.

What's worse is that the average age at which a child is first exposed to pornography is 11 years old.[2] Among 15- to 24-year-olds, approximately 9 million of them will acquire a sexually transmitted disease (STD) each year.[3] Today's teen will be exposed to more than 300,000 advertisements by the age of 19.[4] One such advertisement in San Diego was a billboard promoting two popular television sitcoms. Located a few blocks from several elementary schools, the neon billboard simply read: "Have 'sex' with 'friends!'"

In the midst of such a war against innocence, how are parents to guard the mental, spiritual, and physical health of their children? Odds are, when you were a teenager your parents never offered you a detailed and convincing explanation of the Church's teaching on chastity. Yet here you are as the parent, needing to provide what may never have been given to you—during a time in history that makes purity more difficult for teens than ever before.

While you were growing up, you were probably expected to be abstinent . . . or else. Perhaps your father would brandish a firearm when your dates came over to the house. Such efforts may have instilled fear—and may have kept you in line—but times have changed, and today's youth need far more motivation to maintain their purity.

Although you may feel helpless when it comes to transmitting a message of self-control and purity to your teenager, you have more power than you might imagine.

They're listening

If you're like most parents of teens, you probably feel as if your teenagers would be just as excited to walk through a shopping mall holding your hand or to download your favorite songs onto their iPod as they would be to listen to your advice on chastity.

Don't be so tough on yourself. The National Campaign to Prevent Teen Pregnancy surveyed more than 1,000 teenagers and asked them what the number one factor was in shaping their decisions about sex. Was it their friends, their siblings, sex educators, or the media? Actually, the most common response was "my parents." Interestingly, when the parents were asked how teens would respond to that question, fewer than one in four answered correctly.[5]

The Catholic Church—and, apparently, your teenager—recognizes you as the primary educator of your children when it comes to the topic of sexuality.[6] Neither the state, nor the schools, nor even the Church can claim that responsibility. Not only do you possess that role as a right and a duty, you are also the most qualified for the task. You know your children better than anyone else. In fact, you probably know them better than they know themselves. You know their virtues and vices, their maturity level (or lack thereof), and you have an ability that they often lack—to understand how their sexual behavior today can shape the rest of their lives. You have the power. Make sure you use it!

What's at Stake?

Some adults assume, "I didn't save myself for marriage, and I ended up just fine. Kids today are going to be kids and they're going to do it anyway. Let's be realistic and make sure they have protection." Interestingly, while a parent might have this permissive attitude toward sons, it seldom extends to daughters. Regardless of the double standard, such a cavalier attitude is more naive than realistic because teen promiscuity carries enormous consequences, even if it is done as "safely" as possible. Here's what's at stake:

- The body: Women are especially at risk for disease. A woman is more likely to become infected with STDs than a man, because her reproductive system is more susceptible to infection. Also, a young woman is **more** likely to be infected than an older one because the cervix of a teenage girl is immature and biologically more vulnerable to certain STDs.[7] According to the *Journal of the American Medical Association*, 40 percent of sexually active girls between the ages of 14 and 19 are currently infected with human papillomavirus (HPV), which, even with vaccines, sometimes leads to cervical cancer.[8] As a result of the STD epidemic, diseases of the female reproductive tract have contributed to countless cases of infertility. Boys, too, are contracting STDs at alarming rates and can also suffer life-long consequences as a result.
- The heart: Girls who are sexually active are more than three times as likely to be depressed as girls who are abstinent.[9] Even if a girl experiments with sex once, research shows that she's more likely to feel depressed.[10] The rate of suicide attempts for sexually active girls (aged 12 to 16) is six times higher than the rate for virgins.[11] For these reasons, the *American*

Journal of Preventive Medicine recommends to doctors: "[Girls who are engaging in] sexual intercourse should be screened for depression, and provided with anticipatory guidance about the mental health risks of these behaviors."[12] Sexually active teenage boys also suffer from the emotional consequences of premarital sexual activity. When compared to abstinent teens, young men who are sexually active are more than twice as likely to struggle with depression and are more than eight times as likely to attempt suicide.[13]

- The future: Those who are sexually active prior to marriage have a significantly increased risk of divorce. When a man gets married as a virgin, his divorce rate is 63 percent lower than a non-virgin. For girls, it's 76 percent lower.[14] There could be several reasons why virgins have lower divorce rates. One reason, according to the journal *Adolescent and Family Health*, is that "Those who have premarital sex are more likely to have extramarital sex (affairs)—and extramarital sex contributes to many divorces."[15] In addition to marital problems, the younger a girl is when she becomes sexually active, the more likely she is to live under the poverty level, as well as to experience more breakups, out-of-wedlock pregnancy, and abortion.[16]

- The mind: Teenage sexual activity is detrimental to academic achievement in both boys and girls.

According to a study of 14 thousand teenagers, those who were abstinent in high school were 60 percent less likely to be expelled from school, 50 percent less likely to drop out, and nearly twice as likely to graduate from college.[17] The success was not because the teens avoided pregnancy or came from better families. Rather, the abstinent teens suffered fewer distractions and emotional turmoil, and were prone to show greater impulse control, perseverance, and other positive attitudes. Or simply put: sexually active teens are *not* going to school thinking about math. The researchers noted, "Because they are more successful in school, teen virgins can expect to have, on average, incomes that will be 16 percent higher than sexually active teens from identical socio-economic backgrounds. This will mean an average increase of $370,000 in income over a lifetime."[18]

- The soul: More important than all the risks to a teenager's body, heart, and wallet is the spiritual effect of sin. In 1917, the Blessed Virgin Mary appeared in Fatima, Portugal and delivered a number of messages to three young people. In one of these apparitions, our Lady said, "More souls go to hell because of sins of the flesh than for any other reason." This warning is not new. The Bible states, "Do not be deceived; neither fornicators . . . nor adulterers . . . will inherit the kingdom of God" (1 Cor 6:9-10, NAB).

If we are truly invested in our children and we hope to give them the brightest possible future, we must open our eyes to the fact that times have changed. More is at stake now than ever before when it comes to their choice for chastity.

There is hope

Despite the cultural forces that wage war against innocence, there is good news. Since 1991 teen sexual activity rates have been dropping, and now the majority of high school students are virgins.[19] In fact, between 1991 and 2005 the sexual activity rate of high school boys dropped twice as quickly as that of high school girls![20] Among teens who have already lost their virginity, approximately two-thirds of them wish they had waited longer to have sex.[21]

Make sure to point out these facts to your teenager, because research shows that "[w]hen teenagers believe that their peers have permissive attitudes toward premarital sex or actually engage in sex, then they themselves are more likely to engage in sex."[22] However, if they are aware of a resurgence of moral values among teens, they'll feel encouraged to move in the right direction.

The trend toward chastity is well underway, and even if the mainstream media doesn't seem to have detected the trend, young people are getting louder and prouder about it. In one study, more than 1,000 teens were asked if it was embarrassing to admit that they are virgins. Surprisingly, 75 percent said no.[23] Most of those who said it was embarrassing were under the age of 15. Only 5 percent of older teens (15 - 17 years of age) thought virginity was an embarrassing admission.

A new sexual revolution is underway, as can be seen by the fact that chastity clubs have been founded at many universities, including Harvard, Princeton, and others. Countless public and Catholic high schools have chastity clubs. Perhaps the most encouraging aspect of these movements is that they have been initiated by the students, not the adults.

In one example, a Pennsylvania high school boy initiated a project whereby he and other young men raised enough money to purchase a white rose for every girl on campus. The young men placed flowers on the lockers of all their female classmates, with a bow that read, "You're worth waiting for."

Not long ago, Abercrombie and Fitch began selling women's T-shirts emblazoned across the chest with: "Who needs brains when you have these?" Twenty-four young women from Pennsylvania initiated a "girlcott" of Abercrombie. The protests made local headlines and eventually landed them an appearance on NBC's *Today Show*. In total, the Girlcott story appeared in 21 cable news segments, 312 local TV news markets, six national and international radio spots, 67 regional newspapers, four national newspapers, eight international newspapers, and 23,000 stories on the Web.[24] Within five days of the *Today Show* appearance, Abercrombie and Filth (um Fitch), released a statement agreeing to discontinue the shirt and to meet with the women. A&F was probably surprised when the women arrived at the meeting in business attire with a PowerPoint presentation on how Abercrombie could change for the better.

Meanwhile, an 11-year-old girl sent a letter to the executives at Nordstrom complaining about their lack of modest clothing options. The letter found its way to Pete Nordstrom, the executive vice-president of the company. Executives returned her letter, letting her know that they would be working to educate their purchasing managers and salespeople about the need to offer a greater range of fashion choices for the youth. A brave sixth-grader shaping the decisions of corporate America! Thankfully, she's not alone. Modesty fashion shows have sprung up across the nation, and their popularity is catching the attention of fashion designers.

To the delight of many adults, countless young people are crusading for a return to traditional moral values. As for the teens unfamiliar with the chastity message, many adults may be surprised to hear how receptive they are to it. Most teenagers are accustomed to being told that they're just kids "who are going to do it anyway."

However, when someone tells them that they are capable of heroic sacrifice, they often appreciate the challenge, seeing it as a compliment. Simply to propose chastity to a teenager shows that you renounce the insulting notion that teens are powerless to make the right choices.

Pope John Paul II said that

> young people are always searching for the beauty in love. They want their love to be beautiful. If they give in to weakness, following [worldly] models of behavior . . . in the depths of their hearts they still desire a beautiful and pure love. This is as true of boys as it is of girls. Ultimately, they know that only God can give them this love. As a result, they are willing to follow Christ, without caring about the sacrifices this may entail.[25]

Why are they responding?

Young people are responding to the message of chastity not because it offers them a surefire way to avoid gonorrhea and unwed pregnancy. Rather, they're beginning to see how chastity helps them to experience authentic love. While abstinence is merely a "no" to illicit sex, chastity is a "yes" to something positive. Instead of taking something away from them, chastity has something to offer them. It teaches them to overcome selfishness so that they can be free to love. Because so many teens have suffered through heartache, broken families, and untold amounts of confusion in their relationships, they are pining for something that can offer them hope, meaning, and clarity.

The world, the flesh, and the devil may be opposed to the message of chastity, but we have an advantage that they do not. Young people thirst for love. They want to know what it is, how to recognize the counterfeits, and how to find the real thing. Because the human mind has been made for truth, teens hunger for it. Because their hearts have been created for love, they will not be satisfied with anything less. The beauty of chastity is that it offers the *truth* of God's plan for human sexuality, and frees a person to give and receive authentic *love*.

Lust, on the contrary, leads to self-centeredness. It prevents us from being able to make a gift of ourselves to others and motivates us to take from others instead. Lust deforms our vision—making us see others as objects to be used rather than people to be loved.

For this reason, love is impossible without purity of heart. Since chastity protects us from the self-centeredness of lust, it frees us to look beyond ourselves and to love in a self-giving way. This enables us to become fully human, fully alive, and fully who God created us to be. Chastity does not deny the goodness of our sexuality. It is not a Victorian, prudish idea—quite the reverse. Only the chaste realize the greatness of the gift of human sexuality and treat it with the honor it deserves. When teens begin to grasp this vision of human love, they realize that chastity is not the enemy of love, but rather its guardian.

Be not afraid!

In the midst of today's moral decay and confusion, we must remember the phrase Jesus repeated more than any other in Scripture: "Be not afraid!" You might be holding this book because you are frustrated by the culture at large, because you've lost hope, or because you're reeling from the aftermath of a situation your teen has fallen into. You may feel small as you stand on the frontline, defending your child from the onslaught of the culture wars.

But while you have good reason to be concerned, you also have good reason to hope. You have a message to share with your child about the love she was made for! You have God on your side! Your voice might be quieter than the booming voice of the culture, but it's infinitely mightier. The message of pleasure is like a shallow but noisy stream. The truth runs like a deep, quiet river. When the truth is spoken by a parent, it hits the soul of a child more powerfully and persuasively than the empty noises of the culture ever could.

Moreover, a new sexual revolution is underway, even if it's hard to see it. You have an indispensable role in igniting and sustaining this revolution. The family is the primary means God will use to renew the culture.

Therefore, here are 10 strategies for winning the culture wars in your own home. Some may be novel ideas to you. Others, you may have been doing for years. Indeed, many of the tips that follow were given to us by parents around the country. If you've already been using some of these strategies, we offer them to reinforce you in the times that you may doubt yourself as a parent. You *can* win the battle for your teen's purity, regardless of his or her past! The following 10 points will show you how.

GROUP STUDY QUESTIONS:

1. What do you feel is the greatest threat to the innocence of young people today?
2. Do you think that most parents underestimate the problems associated with promiscuity? Why?
3. What signs have you seen that a culture of purity is spreading?
4. Did your parents present the message of chastity to you? How?
5. Before reading this, what would you have assumed teens would say was the number-one factor in shaping their sexual decisions?

Strategies
to win
the battle

1.

Pray!

"Let us then with confidence draw near to
the throne of grace, that we may receive mercy
and find grace to help in time of need."
(Heb 4:16)

"Pray, hope, and don't worry."
—St. Padre Pio

Many of us think of prayer as a parachute when all else fails. But parents can't afford to lose sight of the spiritual nature of the struggle for purity. After all, sexual behavior can have eternal consequences.

St. Paul said:

> Put on the whole armor of God, that you may be able to stand against the wiles of the devil. For we are not contending against flesh and blood, but against the principalities, against the powers, against the world rulers of this present darkness, against the spiritual hosts of wickedness in the heavenly places. (Eph 6:12)

Christian theologians have speculated that there are nine levels or "choirs" of angels, such as the seraphim, cherubim, thrones, dominions, and so on.[26] The terms "principalities" and "powers" that Paul mentions are also believed to be two of them.

It is interesting that even non-Christians today are happy to consider the presence of angels in our lives. But Scripture tells us that one-third of the angels fell from grace. When the angels fell, they retained their rank of authority and power in the spiritual realm as part of their nature. For example, when any of the seraphim became demons, they began using their spiritual powers to draw souls away from God rather than toward him. An unseen host of angelic beings surround all of mankind and are intertwined with our eternal destiny, yet we live nearly our entire lives unaware.

After reminding Christians to open their eyes to this spiritual reality, Paul asks his readers to pray at all times and to intercede for each other and for him (Eph 6:18-20). If Paul needed prayers in order to do God's will, how much more so do teenagers today need our prayers! The battle for purity is not simply a cultural problem. It is a spiritual war. For the sake of your children, arm yourself.

Pray for them

There are many ways that parents can intercede for their children (as well as their dates, friends, future spouse, etc.). The most fundamental is the daily heart-to-heart conversations with God. We have a God who loves our children more than we ever could. If we want him to bless them, we only have to ask. In the words of Bishop Fulton Sheen, "Millions and millions of favors are hanging from heaven on silken cords, and prayer is the sword that cuts them."[27]

Trusting in the providence of God creates peace in the heart of a parent. St. Paul wrote: "Have no anxiety about anything, but in everything by prayer and supplication with thanksgiving let your requests be made known to God. And the peace of God, which passes all understanding, will keep your hearts and minds in Christ Jesus" (Phil 4:6-7).

The idea of anxiety-free raising of teenagers may seem absurd, but Paul wants us to remember who is ultimately in charge.

Beyond this heart-to-heart dialogue with God, which should be an ordinary part of Christian living, there are many other ways in which a parent can obtain grace for a child. The most powerful form of prayer is the Mass. When you go to Church on Sunday, *make sure to offer the Mass for a specific intention*. You can also attend weekday Masses if you are able. Offer your Masses for the graces your teenager needs most. You also can contact the parish office and request that a Mass be offered specifically for your child. This small effort will reap infinite benefits.

You should also seek the help of religious communities. Call or visit a local convent or monastery of religious sisters or brothers and ask them to pray for your children. With a simple Internet search, you can find addresses for cloistered convents of contemplative nuns. Write to them. Give them the names of your family members, and ask their intercession. The apostle James tell us, "The prayer of a righteous man has great power in its effects" (Jas 5:16).

Look for help from the holiest religious community: heaven. Imagine if you could have met Bl.

Mother Teresa or Pope John Paul II when they were alive. Consider what it would have been like if you had a brief conversation with them and they asked you, "Is there anything you would like me to pray for?" You would pour out your heart to them. Now, imagine if you were invited to be by the bedside of Mother Teresa or Pope John Paul II as they passed away. Could you imagine what it would be like if they turned to you before taking their last breath, and said, "I am about to behold God face-to-face. Is there anything you would like me to ask him for you?" What an honor this would be! Now, consider that this blessing is always available to us, as members of the Mystical Body of Christ.

So, ask the intercession of the angels and saints for your children. Offer novenas, or take up a special devotion to a particular angel or saint. If your son has made a poor decision with regards to his girlfriend, you might ask the intercession of St. Monica. She knows the suffering of a parent's heart: Her son left the Church and fathered a child out of wedlock. She prayed fervently for her son for nearly two decades, and we now know him as St. Augustine. If your daughter has decided to move in with her boyfriend, consider asking St. Margaret of Cortona to pray for her. St. Margaret shacked up with her boyfriend and had a child by him, but she later converted and became a saint. Other saints do not have dramatic conversion stories, but always remained true to

God, such as St. Joseph, St. Therese, St. Dominic Savio, or others. There is no struggle that the saints have not faced themselves, so do not fail to take advantage of their intercessory power as they stand before the throne of God.

Among all the saints, the Church recognizes the unique primacy of the Blessed Virgin Mary. Consider the praises that the other saints said about her: St. Bonaventure proclaimed, "Men do not fear a powerful hostile army as the powers of hell fear the name and protection of Mary."[28] St. John Vianney said, "Only after the Last Judgment will Mary get any rest; from now until then, she is much too busy with her children."[29] Therefore, ask her to pray for your children. One great way to do this is to pray the rosary daily. This takes a mere 15 minutes, and can be done while driving to work or cleaning house. Not only will this serve to sanctify your day, it will also reap a massive amount of grace for your family.

Fast for them

Fasting is a powerful form of Christian prayer. In the Gospel of Mark, Jesus taught his disciples that some demons can only be cast out by both prayer and fasting.[30] While some may choose to fast on merely bread and water for the day, others may wish to skip desserts or snacks between meals. The severity of the sacrifice does not matter as much as the love with which it is offered. With that in mind, make sure you don't fast in a way that is unhealthy or makes you grumpy towards your family. If you want to fast on a regular basis, ask your pastor (and perhaps even your doctor) what kind of fasting is good for you.

To the worldly mind, the concept of fasting would seem absurd. It takes a great amount of faith to imagine that your food intake can spiritually benefit somebody else. But if you believe that prayer works, it is a small step to accept that fasting does as well. Think of it as praying with your body.

Offer it up

Another powerful form of intercession is to offer up your suffering. If you were raised by Catholic parents or attended Catholic grade school, you probably heard a parent or nun telling you to "offer it up." What are they talking about? It can sound like a pious way of saying what they really mean: "Deal with it and don't complain to me." But what does it mean to offer something up? The concept is seen in St. Paul's letter to the Colossians, where he writes, "Now I rejoice in my sufferings for your sake, and in my flesh I complete what is lacking in Christ's afflictions for the sake of his body, that is, the Church" (Col 1:24).

It sounds absurd that Paul could make up what is lacking in the sufferings of Jesus. Did Jesus not suffer enough? What Paul is explaining is that Jesus did not suffer so that we would not have to. He suffered so that we would know *how* to. Some Bible scholars have explained this verse: "Christ's sufferings were, of course, sufficient for our Redemption, but all of us may add ours to his, in order that the fruits of his Redemption be applied to the souls of men."[31] Human suffering has redemptive value, if we take advantage of it. In the words of St. Therese of Lisieux, "Sufferings gladly borne for others convert more people than sermons."[32]

One modern Italian teenager, Chiara Luce Badano, had a profound sense of redemptive suffering. A beautiful girl with a bright future, she was diagnosed with a rare and painful form of bone cancer. Fearless, she often repeated the phrase, "If this is what you want, Jesus, so do I." Like any teenage girl, she loved her hair, but with each lock that fell out she'd pray, "For you, Jesus." Chiara knew that her suffering, offered up to the Father in union with Jesus' suffering, was saving souls. After refusing morphine, she said, "I want to share as much as possible in his suffering on the cross."

Her suffering was immense, but not as immense as her joy, which only increased with her suffering. After one very pain-filled night she said, "I suffered a lot, but my soul was singing." Take a moment to Google pictures of her on her death bed. Her eyes look like pools reflecting the glory of heaven. One of her doctors remarked, "Through her smile, and through her eyes full of light, she showed us that death doesn't exist; only life exists." Cardinal Giovanni Saldarini heard of this amazing teen and visited her in the hospital. Awestruck, he said, "The light in your eyes is splendid. Where does it come from?" Chiara's reply was simple. "I try to love Jesus as much as I can." She also said, "Embraced pain makes one free." She died on October 7, 1990. Her last words were "Goodbye. Be happy because I'm happy." She was only 18, and yet her cause for canonization is already underway.[33]

Suffering can be immense. If we do not understand the value of human suffering, it will crush us. But when we discover its worth, it will lift us and others to heaven. Accepting suffering may not take away its weight, but it does give it meaning. When we embrace the cross, it becomes a purifying fire that sanctifies us. However, if we experience suffering but simply grumble at it, we miss the chance to win inestimable graces for ourselves and others. Failure to offer up suffering to God is like having a winning lottery ticket and never cashing it in.

Most of us won't have to suffer as Chiara did at such a young age. But as a parent of a teen, you probably have plenty of smaller, daily suffering to cash in—a headache, your work, or your dull job as a teen chauffeur. Turn it all into prayer by saying "Jesus, I offer this up for . . ."

Or better yet, start each day with a prayer offering your whole day as a sacrifice to God for a specific intention.

Without downplaying the suffering of fathers, it must be said that mothers suffer in a unique way because they love in a unique way. The maternal bond, formed even prior to birth, allows a mother to experience a profound closeness with her children. When children hurt themselves through poor decisions, a mother internalizes the suffering in a uniquely feminine way. This maternal bond is reflected on a biological level.

Years ago, scientists developed a medical procedure known as "fetal cell sorting" in order to assess the health of an unborn child. When a woman is pregnant, blood cells from the child pass through the placenta and mingle with the blood of the mother. Scientists discovered that by taking blood from an expectant mother and sorting through the cells, they were able to find cells of her unborn child living in her bloodstream. Even more surprising is that they also discovered cells of other children whom the woman had given birth to years before, still flowing in the mother's veins! Scientists have discovered the cells of children living in their mothers 38 years after the children were born.[34] This phenomena, called fetal microchimerism, is well documented in medical literature but is largely unknown by mothers.[35] Interestingly, through a process known as maternal microchimerism, the cells of mothers can also be found in their children.[36]

This minor miracle shared between mothers and their children illuminates the special bond they share throughout life. (On a theological level, it's worth pondering what this discovery says about the union between Jesus and Mary.)

Mothers have a unique capacity to be united with their children. That means they also have a unique capacity to suffer with them and a special role in offering their suffering as prayer for them. Much depends upon how we suffer. As one priest said, "[T]he money to buy souls is suffering, accepted with love. . . . Suffering is a goldmine to exploit for saving souls, for helping missionaries, for being a hidden apostle. What happiness it is to be able to suffer when we cannot act! . . . The Lord has given us a field to work, and we must irrigate it with tears falling from the winepress of sorrow, in order that it may be fruitful."[37]

Be a witness of prayer

Beyond the graces you acquire for your children in prayer, they will also benefit from the witness of your prayer life in general. Recalling his childhood, Pope John Paul II said that he would often find his father, at night or in the early morning, praying silently on his knees. The two read the Bible and prayed the rosary together on a regular basis.[38] The Holy Father described his father as a man "of constant prayer."[39]

Parents, we should ask ourselves: Does my faith leave such an impression? Do my children see me as a person of prayer? Does our faith give us joy? Are we living out the faith in every aspect of our lives? These questions are essential to ask because raising pure teens is not about selling them on one particular issue, but rather on the entire lifestyle of following Christ.

Pray with them

It is not enough to pray *for* our children. We must pray *with* our children. Christianity is not a set of burdensome rules. It is an encounter with the God who loves us. Prayer conveys this reality as it teaches us to encounter him in our daily lives. This responsibility cannot be left to mothers alone, as noted by John Paul II. When speaking to college men before he became pope, he said, "When you are a father . . . 'Go and teach.' When you kneel with your child in prayer: 'Teach!'"[40]

If prayer was not a part of your family upbringing or does not play a significant role in your family life today, it isn't hard to change that. First and foremost, attend Sunday Mass. Sunday Mass isn't a suggestion from God, but a command. Fulfilling it teaches our children to put first things first. (In other words, it teaches them that God is more important than soccer.)

Second, let vocal prayer be a regular part of your family life. Get over your discomfort about prayer. If parents (especially dads) are afraid to talk to God with their children, children will grow up thinking that spirituality doesn't extend beyond the walls of their church. If you don't pray grace before meals, begin doing so. If you already pray grace at meals, try using something beyond the traditional formula of "Bless us, O Lord . . ." Pause to pray for your children's upcoming tests, tryouts, or even their future vocations. Let them see you praying for your spouse as well.

You may also want to consider praying a rosary in the evening with your family after dinner. This is an ideal time, because the family is already in one place, and the practice only takes an additional 15 minutes. If a nearby parish has eucharistic adoration, consider signing up for an hour each week and bringing a different family member with you each time.

Another beautiful form of prayer is listening to God by reading Scripture. Try a bit of the Gospels each day, spending a moment in silence and letting each family member share what God is saying to them through his word. This type of reflective reading of Scripture is called *lectio divina* (divine reading). Pope Benedict XVI said that *lectio divina* "will bring to the Church . . . a new spiritual springtime."[41] There is powerful grace given when we listen to what God has to say and then apply it to our lives.

On one Saturday afternoon each month, consider taking the entire family to the sacrament of reconciliation. After all, it's easy to examine your conscience when you're surrounded by those who know your faults better than anyone! Taking up the habit of frequent confession shows teens that even you, as the parent, need the help of God to overcome your shortcomings.

For a teenager, the habits of personal prayer, Mass, the rosary, and frequent confession need to be developed prior to college life, because such habits are not likely to be fostered by ordinary campus living. In fact, the interior life is essential for anyone to live a pure life, regardless of age. The Church teaches, "Young people especially should earnestly foster devotion to the Immaculate Mother of God, and take as examples the lives of saints and other faithful people, especially young ones, who excelled in the practice of chastity."[42] Or, in the words of St. Philip Neri, "Devotion to the Blessed Sacrament and devotion to the Blessed Virgin are not simply the best way, but in fact the only way to keep purity. At the age of 20 nothing but Communion can keep one's heart pure . . . Chastity is not possible without the Eucharist."[43] It is unfair to expect a person to live a virtuous life without teaching him where to obtain the necessary graces.

When prayers don't seem to work

Teenagers sometimes make decisions that are almost miraculously stupid. Parents' natural tendency is to look for a rationale behind the bad behavior. When nothing seems to add up, they often think, "It's my fault. I should have done things differently. I shouldn't have let him hang out with those friends." Or, "I shouldn't have been so strict. I pushed her away." Don't do this to yourself. The very fact that you're taking the time to read this book should tell you that you are already a loving parent.

Before being too harsh on yourself, ask, "Who is the best parent in the universe?" It's the heavenly Father. Now look at how messed up all of his kids are down here! It's not because he's a defective dad. It's because his children have the gift of free will, and they sometimes don't make the best choices. The same is true of our own children. It is well known that many wayward teens have saintly parents and many saintly teens have wayward parents! It would be wonderful if the sanctity of a parent automatically transferred to his children. Unfortunately, it isn't that simple. But Scripture reassures us, "Train up a child in the way he should go, and when he is old he will not depart from it" (Prv 22:6). That doesn't necessarily mean the child won't depart from it before he gets old, but rather that the seeds you plant will come to fruition in time.

If you've tried all you can do, and you've spent countless hours in prayer for your child with no signs of improvement, do not lose hope. Imagine your prayers welling up like water behind a dam. That concrete wall is your child's free will, which currently stands against all your hopes. You may feel helpless at times, but remember that a persistent drop of water can wear through stone over time. Eventually, the dam will crack under the weight of the grace of your prayers. All the graces you have stored up for your child through your tears and prayers will come flowing into the dry valleys. In the meantime, offer up the suffering, and trust that God will never be outdone in generosity.

In conclusion, Fr. Jean C.J. d'Elbé recommends:

> Say, like one mother I know who was distressed by the conduct of her children, "Jesus, You love them too much not to save them." Thank him in advance for the heaven he is preparing for them because of your prayer, but—and this is very, very important—while you are suffering, wait in peace for the time of Jesus, the time chosen by him to grant your request. He will perhaps make you wait a long time, precisely as a proof of your confidence. Do not disappoint him; tell him, whatever your trial, that with his grace nothing will make you lose your profound peace, because you are sure of him. Add your

sufferings to the apostolate of your prayers united to the prayer of Jesus, which is the Mass. He willed to save the world by suffering. In order to redeem souls with the Savior, you must suffer with him and like him. Your Mass, which is a memorial of Calvary, will be of much more value if you are there at the foot of the cross, or better still, on the cross.[44]

Both authors of this book went through rebellious phases as teenagers, but the prayers and persistence of our parents carried the day, and the root they gave us couldn't be pulled out (much to the devil's dismay).

GROUP STUDY QUESTIONS:

1. Do you have any special ways you pray for your spouse and children?
2. How do you think your spouse would react if you asked him or her to fast with you for your children?
3. Do you pray as a family? If not, what is a concrete way that you can begin?
4. What struggles do you think you'll face in making daily prayer with your family a reality?
5. How do you think daily prayer would affect your family for the better?

2.

Understand their motives.

"I do not understand my own actions. For I do not do what I want, but I do the very thing I hate." (Rom 7:15)

"Our hearts were made for you, O Lord, and they will never rest until they rest in you."
—St. Augustine

In order to raise chaste teens, it's essential to understand why so many young people choose to live unchaste lives. Here are some of the most common motivating forces, and what you can do to counteract them:

Sexual desire

Teenage boys tend to engage in sexual activity for different reasons than girls. For young men, the decision is often motivated by a desire for pleasure. This is not merely a gender stereotype. In her book *The Female Brain*, Louann Brazening, M.D., points out that when a boy is only eight weeks old in his mother's womb, a surge of testosterone begins that kills off cells in the communication center of his brain, while growing more cells in the area of the brain dedicated to sex and aggressiveness.[45] In fact, the area of the male brain dedicated to the sexual drive is more than twice as large as a woman's.[46] This is not to say that females lack sexual desire, but that their desire for sexual intimacy is not fueled primarily by hormones.

St. John says, "I write to you, young men, because you are strong and the word of God remains in you, and you have conquered the evil one [aka: "the devil"]" (1 Jn 2:14). It wouldn't be a stretch to speculate that John was thinking of a young man's battle against sexual sin. The battle can be *that* intense. Therefore, make sure you're doing all you can to help them through the struggle.

Talk to them about their desires

As awkward as this might be for a parent (and a teen), young people need to understand what is going on in their bodies. While a parent might feel qualified to explain to a 14-year-old why he suddenly needs deodorant, more important questions weigh on his heart. For example, "Why would God allow me to experience such intense sexual desires and expect me to remain abstinent?" or "Am I bad for having these desires?" Failure to address such questions can lead to profound confusion, a feeling that something is somehow wrong with them, and eventually, burnout.

An unhealthy or puritanical answer to a teen's questions can make him feel guilty for having such desires—as if the longing for sexual intimacy is inherently wrong. The Church states in this regard that,

> [P]arents should offer well-reasoned arguments about the great value of chastity . . . They will answer clearly, without giving excessive importance to pathological sexual problems. *Nor will they give the false impression that sex is something shameful or dirty*, because it is a great gift of God who placed the ability to generate life in the human body, thereby sharing his creative power with us. Indeed, both in Scripture

(cf. Song 1-8; Hos 2; Jer 3:1-3; Ez 23, etc.) and in the Christian mystical tradition, conjugal love has always been considered a symbol and image of God's love for us.[47]

God is the architect of our bodies, and he is the one who planted within us the yearning to become one flesh with someone else. Therefore, it is essential for teens (especially boys) to know that it is perfectly healthy and normal to experience strong sexual desires. Giving this information is not an endorsement of lust. Lust is a sinful and selfish desire to use another for one's own gratification. Sexual desire, on the other hand, is a biological urge that takes on a moral value depending upon how we react to it. Teens who are not taught the difference between lust and sexual desire will not be able to integrate their sexuality with their faith. The two will always seem in opposition to one another. If they want to be close to God, they will assume that they are failing him as long as sexual intimacy seems appealing. They may even come to the point of assuming that chastity requires the annihilation of sexual desire. Because a teen's sexual appetite can be so strong, the possibility of sanctity would seem impossible. When this happens, it's hard to blame him for feeling discouraged. On the other hand, if he understands that his desires have been given by God but have been affected by original sin, he will be able to make sense of his desires.

Keep them busy

Another way to help them deal with desire is to keep them busy with positive things. Some battles are best won by avoiding them all together. Nothing leads to lust like boredom! St. Robert Bellarmine warned, "Flee idleness, for no one is more exposed to such temptations than he who has nothing to do."[48][44] When a teen has too much free time, it is not surprising that he would turn to pleasure as a form of entertainment. Therefore, encourage your teen to become active in sports, school activities, clubs, youth group, or work. If he has three hours of soccer practice after school, that's three fewer hours to surf the Internet or spend time alone with a girlfriend.

Looking for love

Many young women become sexually active out of the desire to feel accepted and wanted—especially as they experience the natural need for affirmation that accompanies their physical and emotional development. Many are starving for love and yearning for security. This is especially the case when she lacks a close and positive relationship with her father. When a young woman experiences a broken relationship with her father (often because of abuse or divorce), she will look elsewhere for male approval. One high school girl admitted in an e-mail to a friend why she had slept with numerous boys: "I was only doing it because I had this total and complete lack of love in my life." The allure of sexual activity for teens (especially young women) can be overwhelming when they feel unloved or deprived of affection. Teens long for love. If they are not receiving it, they become determined to find it, often in the wrong ways.

Make sure they find love at home

Home needs to be a safe haven of love and acceptance for your child. Teens today live in a ruthless world. Internet bullying, gossip, sarcasm, and all the social pressures that a teen may experience leave them thirsting for praise and affirmation. If they feel ignored or rejected at home, this only primes them for illicit forms of affection and false love. Therefore, it is essential that parents praise their children at least twice as often as they criticize them. As difficult as it may be, do your best to always express love in your face, even when you have to correct them.

As one priest said in a five-second homily, "Negative humor is from the pits of hell. Keep it there!"[49] Married couples know that sarcasm destroys intimacy, and the same is true in parent-child relationships. Teens must hear "I love you," "I'm proud of you," "You look pretty (or handsome)" and other such things. Otherwise, they're not likely to believe it. If you build them up at home, then when a teenage boy says to your daughter, "You look beautiful. I love you," she will think, "I know. My dad's been telling me that since I was in diapers."

Physical affirmation

Teens also need physical affirmation. Although they may cringe and squirm whenever you come near them, do not stop hugging and kissing them. Don't forget the simple touches, such as a hand on a shoulder or a little blessing on their forehead before bed. If you have multiple children, be sure to spend time focusing on each of them in this way. Especially if you were raised in a home where affection was not a common form of communication, you must choose to break from that mold.

Time

Finally, in our busy world, it's important to remember that "quantity time" is just as important as "quality time." Many children spell "love" in this way: T-I-M-E. Spend time together as a family, whether it's family dinners, prayer, or recreational activity. No matter how strong your teen's biological desires may be, researchers have discovered that family values are stronger, and only time spent together can communicate your family's values to your child. According to Drs. Joe McIlhaney and Freda McKissic Bush, when the sexual activity of teens was studied in relation to hormone levels, "home environment had greater influence on behavior than hormone levels and if parent-child relations were good, hormone levels do not seem to matter at all regarding risky sexual behavior."[50] Without question, when teens feel connected to their family, they are less likely to be sexually active.[51]

Caving in to peer pressure

As they mature, young people experience a natural curiosity with regard to their sexuality. Add to that pressure from friends and dates and you have a volatile situation. Many teens feel obligated to give away their virginity before leaving for college if they have not already. Their friends may even tell them to "just get it over with"—an expression that sounds more appropriate for getting wisdom teeth removed.

Beyond the pressure from friends, both males and females experience pressure from their dates. It used to be that girls had to worry about boys pressuring them to engage in sexual behavior. While this concern still exists, today's teenage boys now have to deal with sexually aggressive girls. Whether through sexual text messages, suggestive dancing, or sensual flirting, many young women are taking the offensive when it comes to catching a boy's attention. Unless he is deeply motivated to maintain his purity, if he

receives a sexual solicitation from a female class-
mate, he'll more than likely take her up on the offer.
Such "relationships" rarely last, but the damage
caused by them endures.

Let them know they are not alone

Because of the many external pressures encouraging
promiscuity, it's crucial that young people understand that they're not alone when they choose to
be chaste. As we said above, a "pure revolution" is
underway. Share that good news with your child.
Believe it or not, two-thirds of high school students
are not currently sexually active—and if teens are
aware that they're not alone, they're more likely to
make the right choices.[52]

It's also important to offer them pure role models.
Many young men who become sexually active in high
school lack a positive male role model. If you look at
the people teenage boys admire, they are often athletes
or musicians (who rarely set a positive example when
it comes to living the virtue of chastity). Furthermore,
these people are not part of their daily lives. Therefore,
the Church teaches, "Parents should always strive to
give *example and witness* with their own lives to fidel-
ity to God and one another in the marriage covenant.
Their example is especially decisive in adolescence,
the phase when young people are looking for *lived*

and attractive behavior models."[53] Beyond your own example, make the effort to expose your teen to role models, such as saints, youth ministers, relatives, or even athletes and musicians who practice chastity. Yes, they do exist! (See the resource section.)

Caving in to the culture

Everyone has an innate ability to distinguish right from wrong. Despite our attraction to sin, it's ingrained in human nature to feel a twinge of conscience when sinning. But this natural response is being muted by a culture that denies the existence of sin, or at best doesn't see it as all that harmful—especially sexual sin. As a result, young people often end up falling into promiscuity for no significant reason or motive other than, "Hey, why not?"

The cultural trend toward amorality is rooted in two "philosophies:" relativism and hedonism. It's crucial that we have a firm grasp on the culture in which our children live, so let's take a look at what these philosophies are and why they're wrong.

Relativism

The essence of relativism is the denial of the existence of objective truth. Therefore, moral relativism is the belief that there's no such thing as right and wrong. All that exists are valid opinions that vary from person to person.

Such a mentality causes a loss of the sense of sin. In fact, the only "sin" would be to go against my personal values or to violate my private system of morality. In other words, the Ten Commandments become multiple choice.

This philosophy has become so widespread that prior to becoming pope, Benedict XVI spoke of a "dictatorship of relativism."[54] He also referred to relativism as "the greatest problem of our time."[55]

The flaws of relativism are obvious to those who look closely at the concept. First, it doesn't work in real life. A bank robber won't get his charges dropped if he argues that his heist did not violate his personal values. His opinion has no bearing on the fact that some things are objectively wrong. Second, relativism doesn't work as a philosophy. It contradicts itself by making the claim that "it's true for everyone that nothing is true for everyone."

But the thing that makes relativism "the greatest problem of our time" isn't just that it leads to heated debates in the halls of a university's philosophy department. Relativism has led to widespread moral confusion and countless ruined lives, and it's easy to see why.

Relativism removes any higher principles that should guide our moral choices—leaving young people with moral compasses that only point to themselves. Benedict said that relativism "leaves as the ultimate criterion [for moral decision making] only the self with its desires."[56] Instead of learning how to discern right from wrong, young people raised in a relativist society are taught how to "clarify their own values."

When faced with a moral dilemma such as "Should I have sex with my girlfriend?," instead of asking, "Is this right?" relativists are more prone to ask, "Does this *feel* right?" or "Do I *feel* ready?" This approach to reality has led countless young people to personal ruin through promiscuity, drug abuse, and a myriad of other destructive choices that might have felt good for the moment.

When we offer our children acceptance without guidance or teach them ethics without truth, we are morally abandoning them. The sad irony is that this abandonment usually happens in the name of love. But love without truth (much like truth without love) is cruelty. In the words of Benedict, "*Only in truth does charity shine forth*, only in truth can charity be authentically lived. . . . Without truth, charity degenerates into sentimentality. Love becomes an empty shell, to be filled in an arbitrary way. In a culture without truth, this is the fatal risk facing love."[57]

Hedonism

When objective truth is denied in a society, people still need a motive to guide their behavior. In the absence of moral standards, the reward of pleasure begins to reign. This results in the problem of hedonism.[58]

Simply put, hedonism is the philosophy that the pursuit of carnal pleasure is of utmost importance, and that it's either pointless or impossible to try to restrain your urges. In today's secular culture, many people adopt this mentality. As St. Thomas Aquinas pointed out, "No man can live without delight. That is why a man deprived of spiritual joy goes over to carnal pleasures."[59] The connection between relativism and hedonism isn't hard to see. If there is no such thing as right and wrong, why not indulge every pleasure?

In our modern world, hedonism doesn't look the same as it did for the barbarians. It's sophisticated. It considers self-mastery (the ability to say "no") to be unhealthy repression—a borderline mental condition. It denies the existence of sin, and considers sexual morality to be a hindrance to personal fulfillment.

In today's culture, people risk suffering and death (STDs) to gain pleasure for themselves and choose death for others (abortion and euthanasia) to avoid suffering. It's no wonder that John Paul II considered hedonism to be a pillar of the "culture of death."[60]

Relativism and hedonism touch on every area of teen culture—from the music they listen to, to the Web sites at their fingertips, to the principles behind sex education, to the permissiveness of their friends' parents—and they leave teens with no sense of sin and no motivation to avoid it.

How do you battle a cultural problem?
Create a different culture!

Unfortunately, the culture at large is more difficult to contend with than the junior-higher who just showed up at your door wanting to take your daughter to a dance. You can scare him away with a long stare and an awkward silence. The only way to preserve your teen from contact with the culture is to purchase a small island and move your family to it, which for most of us isn't an option.

Teens living in a culture that celebrates sexual permissiveness and perversion need to be drawn into a culture that celebrates beauty, goodness, and truth. But where to find such a culture? At home and at church.

In response to the culture at large, we need to be very deliberate in our efforts to create an atmosphere that encourages traditional values at home. A few generations ago, when the culture expected chastity of young people, families didn't have to work as hard to raise virtuous children. One could learn chastity by "cultural osmosis." Today, if you are lukewarm, your child will probably end up freezing. We need to make sure our children grasp the religious and moral truths that we presume are obvious. To do this, we must practice the simple things that show our children who we are as people of faith—like family prayer and Sunday worship, quality time together, service, respectful speech, and connecting with other solid families.

Second, your local church should provide a subculture for your teen to enter into. If your parish doesn't have youth ministry, encourage the pastor to invest in it. If a youth group exists, send your teen! Wonderful things are happening in the world of Catholic youth ministry. For example, check out deadtheologianssociety.com or lifeteen.com to see two excellent forms of youth evangelization. Both Web sites provide lists of active parishes that use their programs. Many teens also enjoy attending youth conferences to give their faith a boost. For example, 40 thousand teens participate in more than a dozen Steubenville youth conferences every summer. (Visit franciscanyouth.com for more information.) More than 20 thousand teens participate in the bi-annual National Catholic Youth Conference (NCYC). At the 2009 convention, 22 thousand teens knelt in eucharistic adoration, and then processed behind the Blessed Sacrament through the streets of Kansas City, Missouri.

Teens have an inherent desire to rebel (as you may have noticed once or twice). In a culture that is becoming ever more anti-Christian and anti-chastity, an increasing number of teens are finding that holiness is the ultimate form of rebellion. In a self-serving culture, many teens are choosing to serve others on mission trips and in homeless shelters. To the surprise and delight of many adults, teens who are submerged in an irreverent culture will actually gravitate toward ancient practices of piety! Today's Catholic teens think incense and chant are cool! In a culture steeped in promiscuity, many are proud of their choice to wait.

When teens make faith the foundation of their lives, everything begins to fall into place. A recent survey of thousands of U.S. teens revealed that religiously active teens are less likely to be sexually active, smoke, drink, and use marijuana.[61] They are even less likely to waste time watching TV during the week and are much less likely to watch pornography and R-rated movies than non-religiously active teens.[62] Most importantly, teens surveyed said that religion helps them in "making good decisions, providing a sense of hope and purpose in life, motivating them to be moral and altruistic, and helping them get through hard circumstances."[63] In short, faith, on the deepest level, has proven to provide the motive, community support, and the empowerment young people need to live a life of virtue.

The above list of factors that shape a teen's behavior is certainly incomplete. However, the more you learn about what motivates teens to succumb to temptations, the more able you will be to prevent their fall.

GROUP STUDY QUESTIONS:

1. When it comes to raising pure teens, how have you found that raising boys differs from raising girls? In what ways is it easier or more challenging?

2. What are ways that you keep your teen busy, so as to avoid idleness?

3. In what ways have you seen hope in today's teens?

4. What can you do to build a culture that promotes chastity in your home?

5. If your parish has a good youth ministry, how can you get your child more involved? If not, what can you do to surround him with positive peer pressure and good role models?

3.

Teach your teen to say "YES."

"I came that they may have life, and have it abundantly."
(Jn 10:10)

"Chastity is the sure way to happiness."
—Pope John Paul II

Researchers of the adolescent brain have discovered that teenagers base their behavioral decisions primarily upon rewards rather than upon consequences.[64] Therefore, if a teenager asks, "Why should I save sex for marriage?" it won't be effective to respond, "If you don't, you'll get pregnant, die of an STD, and go to hell." Teens often think they are invincible, and so such threats will have little effect upon them.

In order to be chaste, a teen needs to see the benefits of a chaste life. Otherwise, chastity offers nothing. It will be seen as merely the absence of physical intimacy. But a void isn't enough to motivate someone to make a choice against one of the greatest temptations mankind has ever known. Therefore, teens need to realize that chastity is not just about saying "no" to herpes and unwed pregnancy. Chastity is about saying "yes" to authentic love and relationships, "yes" to God's plan for our lives, and "yes" to reaching our full potential as creatures made by Love (God) and for love.

Many people have tried to scare their children away from premarital sex and failed. It's true that premarital sex should scare us. It carries grave consequences that your child needs to realize. However, if a young person equates premarital sex with love, a fear of disease won't keep them from it. Many people would rather be dead than unloved. That's why it's crucial to show the connection of chastity to love and to reveal lust for what it is—the counterfeit of love.

What is love?

It can be difficult to convince teens, who are prone to thinking with their emotions, that premarital sex is *not* loving. After all, it *feels* loving, doesn't it? Lustful acts can even be referred to as "making love."

To convince them otherwise, we need to teach them the meaning of love. Contrary to popular belief, love is not a feeling, though feelings often accompany it. Simply put: Love is willing and doing what is good for someone else.[65] Sometimes this doesn't feel good at all. The greatest expression of love is to lay down your life for the sake of another.[66] Jesus showed us this love on the cross, and while it didn't "feel good," it was the most profound act of love in human history.

Armed with this genuine definition of love you can bring up the many risks of premarital sex to show your child why lust is the opposite of love. Although often accompanied by loving feelings, lustful actions put the physical, emotional, and spiritual life of someone else at risk. That is not love! If you love someone, you want to do what is good for them. You won't risk their future marriage, their reputation, their health, their financial welfare, their relationship with their parents, an untimely pregnancy, and their relationship with

God. In short, if you love someone you won't do what is bad for them, even if it feels good.

If a young woman understands the difference between lust and love, she'll reject lust not only because it risks her well-being, but because it threatens her ability to experience authentic love. Many relationships have lasted for years, sustained by physical passion, only for a young woman to later realize that she was being used. Some couples even enter into marriage with passionate relationships, only to realize years later that they barely know the person to whom they said "I do."

Young men, who often see sex as a rite of passage to manhood, need to be taught that authentic love makes someone a real man. Being able to lay down your life and desire to do what is good for someone else (even at the risk of being mocked for it in the locker room) makes you truly masculine. Using someone makes you less of a man—more like an animal than a man.

Sacrificial love is not easy. The Church reminds us, however, that "[t]he love revealed by Christ 'which the apostle Paul celebrates in the First Letter to the Corinthians . . . is certainly *a demanding love*. But this is precisely the source of its beauty: By the very fact that it is demanding, it builds up the true good of man and allows it to radiate to others.'"[67]

Therefore, when you point out the dangers of pre-marital sex to your child, do so primarily to reveal lust for what it is—the opposite of love, an imitation of love. If teens understand chastity as the way to discover authentic love, they'll find it more attractive than the allure of momentary pleasure—because we were made for love, not lust. While we can overcome our temptations to lust, we can't escape our longing for authentic love any more than we can escape who we are.

The Church reminds parents that

> [t]hey must insist on the positive value of chastity and its capacity to generate true love for other persons. This is the most radical and important moral aspect of chastity. Only a person who knows how to be chaste will know how to love in marriage or in virginity. . . . The objective of the parents' educational task is to pass on to their children the conviction *that chastity in one's state in life is possible and that chastity brings joy.*[68]

A revolution of love

In our ministry as public speakers, we are able to witness how teens respond to the life-giving message of chastity. At the end of an hour-long assembly on purity, the response is consistently overwhelming: standing ovations, break-up text messages being sent before our talk is even finished, countless e-mails telling us we've not only influenced their decision for purity but changed their lives.

Because teens have a tendency to play it cool with their parents, you probably won't get a standing ovation, regardless of how positively you present the message of chastity to them. But you'll make more of an impact than we ever could in an hour-long assembly.

If teens fail to grasp the connection between chastity and love, they'll come to see purity as the enemy of passion, an unhealthy act of repression. This negative perception will most likely end in a rejection of chastity, despite all the risks that go along with that choice.

That is exactly what happened to Hugh Hefner, founder of *Playboy* and a major force behind the sexual revolution. Reflecting on his upbringing, he said, "Our family was Prohibitionist, Puritan in a very real sense." He was taught that sex was "for procreation *only* and the rest was sin." In other words, he wasn't taught about its beauty as a unifying force for a married couple. He may have been taught that chastity prevented sin, but he wasn't shown that it also makes love possible. He also said that this Puritanism extended to all of his family interactions: "There was absolutely no hugging or kissing in my family."[69]

The end result was a radical rejection of chastity. "There was a point in time when my mother, later in life, apologized to me for not being able to show affection," he said. "That was, of course, the way I'd been raised. I said to her, 'Mom, you couldn't have done it any better. And because of the things you weren't able to do, it set me on a course that changed my life and the world.'"[70]

Just as his sexual revolution was founded on a distorted idea of human sexuality, a new sexual revolution must be founded upon the truth. *Chastity is not about obeying a litany of rules so that you don't go to hell. It's about wanting heaven for the person you love.* It is not an obstacle to freedom. It trains us in human freedom because it makes us free to love and to desire the good of another, without being controlled by lust.

GROUP STUDY QUESTIONS:

1. Was chastity explained in this positive way to you? How did you perceive chastity as a teen?

2. Do you think you've clearly explained the benefits of a pure life to your teen? Do they grasp the connection between chastity and love?

3. What are some other ways parents can communicate the benefits of chastity?

4. In addition to talking about it, how else can you communicate to a young man that chastity is a path to true manhood?

5. How can being affectionate with your children strengthen your message? Do displays of affection come naturally to you? Did they for your parents?

4.

Be a parent first and not a buddy.

"Guard what has been entrusted to your care."
(1 Tm 6:20)

"The family is placed at the center of the great
struggle between good and evil, between life and
death, between love and all that is opposed to love."
—Pope John Paul II

Raising teenagers can sometimes feel like walking a tightrope. You want to raise responsible children without being too lenient or strict. You may think, "If I'm too demanding, my teens might rebel. But if I'm too lax with my rules, then I'll fail to protect them." And while it's important to be a friend to your child, it's crucial that you don't do so at the cost of their safety.

Teens have many friends, but only one set of parents. For that reason, your authority in their life is irreplaceable. While playing the cop isn't as fun as being a friend to your child, it's one of the most profound forms of love that a mom or dad can offer. Therefore you should feel proud of yourself if you've repeatedly heard the phrase, "Everyone else gets to go to the movie, the party, etc." If your teenager is moping, opposing your rules, throwing an occasional tantrum, giving you guilt trips, and threatening to disown you, you can be sure that you're a wonderful parent. That's just their way of thanking you.

While teens often view their parents' rules as an expression of domestic tyranny, you can be sure they'll eventually show you their gratitude. You just have to wait about a decade to see it. It will arrive in the form of a phone call, once they're married with children, asking how they're supposed to raise your grandchildren. Until that call arrives, be patient and don't doubt yourself. When writing about her parents, St. Therese of Lisieux stated with deep gratitude, "God gave me a father and mother more worthy of heaven than of earth."[71] This quote is now the epitaph above their graves.

To avoid slipping into the habit of becoming a buddy before a parent, here are a number of strategies to help you keep your child safe:

Protect them from themselves

As you know, your child is not yet an adult. This is a neurological fact. For that reason, your child should not be treated or trusted as an adult. To do so would be unfair to him, despite his claims to the contrary.

This might come as no surprise to you, but your child's brain is an incomplete project. It used to be thought that our brains were fully developed much earlier than they are. However, researchers explain, "It now appears the brain continues to change into the early 20s with the frontal lobes, responsible for reasoning and problem solving, developing last."[72]

This frontal lobe is the part of the brain that helps your teen make responsible decisions. Because it's underdeveloped in teens, they've been known on occasion to make less-than-wise decisions, such as trying to see how far they can drive your car with their eyes closed. So, the next time your teen seems to have a brain-lapse in judgment, and you are inspired to ask the age-old question, "What were you thinking?," his honest answer might be, "I wasn't!" In the words of Jay Giedd, neuroscientist at the National Institute of Mental Health, "It's sort of unfair to expect [teens] to have adult levels of organizational skills or decision making before their brain is finished being built."[73]

That's why God provides parents. Because many teens are blind to the dangers of co-ed sleepovers, dating older people, or spending time at a date's house without supervision, every parent must frequently intervene with the use of every teen's least favorite word: "No."

Protect them from their hormones

In addition to brains that are under construction, teens also have raging hormones. This sounds like a dangerous combination, and it is. This is especially true for boys. During the teen years, boys have 20 times more testosterone than girls.[74] For this reason, girls cannot afford to be ignorant of the biological factors at play. While a girl might see her tight outfit as cute, a teen boy sees things from a different perspective. While a girl may think that snuggling while watching a movie is an end in itself, the boy may see it as an open door to become more physical. If young women are not conscious of these differences, they can easily end up in compromising (and sometimes dangerous) situations. Parents need to make their girls aware of this reality.

It cannot be overlooked, however, that many of today's teenage girls have become more aggressive than the boys. Parents also need to equip their young men with the ability to say "no" to forward girls, primarily by telling their sons to avoid them altogether.

Despite the development occurring in an adolescent brain and their raging hormones, it's important to remember that teens still have the capacity to make good choices. Despite all neurological and hormonal disadvantages, teens have fully formed human souls with powerful wills that are capable of doing the right thing even when faced with great temptation. They just need a little extra help from you to stay out of temptation's way.

For example, when he asks if he can study with his girlfriend behind a closed door, the answer is "no." If your teen asks, "How far is too far?," tell them, "As soon as the door shuts and you're alone behind it with your boyfriend or girlfriend, you've gone too far." If they want to get married one day, you could also invite them to consider how far they would want some other person going with their future husband or wife. No matter how good your children are, it's necessary to set limits and keep them out of the near occasion of sin.

Network with other parents

One of the most effective ways to keep your child out of a near occasion of sin is parent networking. Don't be afraid to pick up the phone to verify that your child is, in fact, going where he said he was going and that parents will be there. Even the best teens can get into bad situations if parents aren't around. Should you have serious doubts about the safety of your teens, you can install GPS software into their cell phones to monitor their whereabouts (and even how fast they're driving)!

It's also crucial that you know and trust the parents whose homes your children will be visiting. As you know, some parents don't seem to have a problem with their teens drinking, doing drugs, and having sex—as long as they are doing it "safely" at home. Such adults are a great danger to teens because they don't seem to realize that incomplete brain development, surging hormones, and alcohol create a perfect storm that leads to nothing but trouble. Therefore, if you feel uneasy about a friend's parents, ask questions and then follow your intuition. Your parental instincts are correct more often than you think.

Teens will never thank you for forbidding them from doing something. But an argument with your teen is easier to deal with than the damage that can be caused by a child who makes bad choices. Remember, it only takes a moment of trauma to make years of counseling necessary—and the house with a parent who permits partying and promiscuity is an invitation for sexual trauma.

Be aware of the danger of sexual abuse

A 2005 survey of 9th–12th graders revealed that "10.8 percent of girls and 4.2 percent of boys from grades 9–12 were forced to have sexual intercourse at some time in their lives."[75] The dangers for young women only increase in college.[76]

Few adults realize the prevalence of sexual abuse today because victims typically hide their pain out of fear or shame. As a result, the crimes are simply never reported.[77] Such secrecy is especially common in male victims.[78] For this reason, parents must take every measure to help their children to feel safe and secure when discussing such matters. This education begins in early childhood, when discussing private areas of the body, but must continue in an age-appropriate manner through adolescence so that teens know that they can always come to you without fear of judgment. Countless teenage victims of sexual abuse think, "I can't tell my parents. They would blame me for what happened, and I don't want them to look at me differently." Even if such fears are untrue in reality, teens need constant reassurance that they are loved unconditionally to overcome such insecurities.

The vast majority of perpetrators of sexual abuse are not strangers, but friends, relatives, acquaintances, and dates—many of whom seemed trustworthy.[79] This does not mean you should develop an unhealthy fear of others, but that you should keep a healthy eye on everyone—much like you do with the cars next to you on the freeway. The tragically high number of victims also means you need to be aware of the signs of sexual abuse, like sudden behavioral and emotional changes, unusual bruises, the onset of sleeping disorders, eating disorders, or depression. When sexual abuse has occurred, it is best to notify the police and press charges, so that the abuser can be stopped from hurting others.

The wounds caused by sexual abuse cannot be ignored. Healing needs to take place with the help of a counselor, the support of loved ones, and perhaps a spiritual director. If the emotional trauma is not addressed, it will affect your child for the rest of his life. Girls who have suffered sexual abuse are more likely to develop a variety of psychological disorders such as bulimia and depression and are more likely to commit suicide in adulthood.[80] They're also more than four times as likely to abuse drugs or alcohol as adults.[81] Parents can't afford to be in denial or to downplay what some teens have experienced. If faced with courage, the process of healing from sexual abuse will form your child into an adult of depth, strength, and compassion—one who will be able to empathize with others. God can bring goodness even out of the greatest darkness. Never lose hope.

Get involved at school events, especially dances

As an involved parent, you can have a great impact on the nature of your child's school environment. For example, chaperone a dance. You may be aware that the phenomena once known as "dirty dancing," is now referred to as "bumping and grinding," "booty dancing," or "juking." Chaperones and faculty members often attempt in vain to break up mobs of students engaging in behavior on the dance floor that hardly resembles dancing. The problem has become such a widespread issue in Catholic and public schools alike that many high schools no longer have dances. It's ironic that schools expect the events to be modest when they have hundreds of immodestly dressed teens huddling in a dark gym for several hours listening to music, most of which glorifies meaningless sex.

Before it gets to this point, you can intervene in several ways. Encourage the school to host "theme dances" such as disco or '80s music, so that the students will not hear the music that encourages immodest dancing. Second, if the school chooses to use modern music, insist that the songs be screened beforehand. Third, encourage the school to have ample lighting during the dances—spotlights if necessary. Fourth, encourage the school to enact a zero-tolerance policy on inappropriate dancing. In other words, when the bumping and grinding begins, the music stops. Fifth, encourage the school to enforce a strict dress code. Some schools will hang posters on campus several weeks before the dances, showing the girls which types of dresses will be accepted, and which will not. If a girl shows up with an inappropriate outfit, she has a choice to leave or stay. If she wishes to stay, she will be offered a garment to be worn over her dress. Since most girls go to painstaking measures to look perfect for dances, they'll choose a modest outfit beforehand, instead of taking the risk of having their efforts ruined by having to wear a cardigan sweater donated by their English teacher. Lastly, chaperone the dances. Even if bumping and grinding persists, your teen is much less likely to take part in it knowing mom or dad is watching like a hawk from across the room.

Monitor friends and fun

Another strategy to help them avoid occasions of sin is to make your house the fun place to be. If you have space in your home, create a game-room with a pool table, video games, ping-pong, and anything else that will keep teens busy. Supply copious amounts of soda and food. Food and fun will keep them coming to your place. And the more time they spend at your place, the less you need to worry about them. But it never hurts to make sporadic visits to check up on them, making sure they have enough chastity . . . I mean . . . food.

Also, be on guard against friends who could be a negative influence. To minimize such friendships, make opportunities for your teen to hang out with the friends you prefer. For example, you could ask your son, "Do you want to invite Luke to go skiing with us this weekend?" That way, you're opening the door for them to form deeper friendships with those who will be a good influence.

How do you know who to keep away from your child? Luckily, teens often make it clear if they are going to be a bad influence. You just have to keep your eyes open, ask questions, and again, follow your gut. In nature, animals often have bright colors if they are poisonous. A predator would overlook the florescent colors of a poison-dart frog at his peril. The prey wants everyone to see that they are dangerous. The same is true of many teens. They often make it easy to see when they are social poison for others. It may be communicated through a lack of eye contact or a bad attitude toward you. Or, it may be as clear as the clothes they wear. One new t-shirt says, "I'm the Person Your Parents Are Afraid Of"! If someone is sending the message that you should be afraid of them by the way they dress, talk, carry themselves, or by the music they listen to—then be afraid and keep your child away from him.

Unfortunately, it's not always so obvious. That's why it is helpful when you befriend the parents of your children's friends. Having an extra pair of eyes on your teen is always beneficial. If they are also responsible adults, then there's the added benefit that your child will witness another functional family. And your teen will be less likely to treat you as if you're the only parent in your ZIP code that actually enforces a curfew.

GROUP STUDY QUESTIONS:

1. How do you handle the situation when your teen protests against your boundaries?
2. How do you handle the situation when he breaks your rules?
3. Do you go out of your way to network with other involved and responsible parents? What are ways parents can do this?
4. Have you ever needed to confront another parent's lack of concern for dangerous situations, such as a co-ed slumber party or senior weekend at the shore?
5. How do you balance your teen's desire for freedom and maturity without being too lenient or strict?

5.

Beware of sex education.

"For this is the will of God, your sanctification: that you abstain from unchastity; that each one of you know how to take a wife for himself in holiness and honor, not in the passion of lust like heathen who do not know God."
(1 Thes 4:3-5)

"Christ is found particularly in the field of sexual morality, because it is here that Christ makes demands on men."
—Pope John Paul II

Many parents assume that classroom sex education exists to help the students avoid pregnancy and STDs. Most would be horrified to learn what is often being taught.

SIECUS (Sexuality Information and Education Council of the United States), Planned Parenthood, and Advocates for Youth are dominant forces behind the materials in sex-education programs. SIECUS has trained thousands of sex educators, and recommends that 5- to 8-year-olds should be taught about masturbation and that 9- to 12-year-olds should be instructed about mutual masturbation and oral sex.[82] They even suggest that high school students should be taught various forms of sexual activity, such as: bathing together, oral, vaginal, or anal intercourse, and the use of pornography to enhance sexual experiences alone or with a partner.[83]

The sex-ed curriculum *Focus on Kids* is designed for children as young as nine. The teacher's guide tells teachers, "State that there are other ways to be close to a person and show you care without having sexual intercourse. Ask youth to brainstorm ways to be close. The list may include holding hands, body massage, bathing together, masturbation, sensuous feeding, fantasizing, watching erotic movies, reading erotic books and magazines."[84] It also recommends "condom hunts" at local markets and a condom race to see who can apply the condom fastest. The curriculum *Becoming a Responsible Teen* is designed for 14- to 18-year-olds, and suggests that students make a trip to the grocery store to examine the different kinds of lubricants for condom use.[85] Both of these programs were promoted by the Centers for Disease Control!

Equally deplorable programs are also being pushed internationally through the United Nations. For example, their International Guidelines on Sexuality Education imposes sex education on children beginning at age five. Grade-schoolers are to be systematically indoctrinated on such topics as abortion rights, sexual liberation, and homophobia. This demonstrates that proponents of sex education are not primarily focused on preventing STDs and unwanted pregnancy. Their ultimate goal is to spread their worldview of human sexuality and stamp out traditional moral values.

Unbeknownst to many parents, Planned Parenthood often sets up shop in schools in order to teach children about *their* version of the birds and the bees. Dr. Miriam Grossman's book, *You're Teaching My Child What?*, outlines how Planned Parenthood workers "'instruct parents to tell 5-year-olds about intercourse, though explaining orgasm can wait until he's finished kindergarten.' And for sadomasochism? Educators can send teen girls to a Web site that says, 'Though it may seem painful, those involved find the pleasure outweighs the pain.'"[86]

The ACLU and the federally funded (i.e. by your tax dollars) Planned Parenthood are major players behind the growing anti-abstinence trend. They see themselves as liberators standing on the front line in a war against traditional sexual ethics. According to Planned Parenthood, "Abstinence-only education is one of the religious right's greatest challenges to the nation's sexual health. But it is only one tactic in a broader, longer-term strategy . . . [T]he 'family values' movement has won the collaboration of governments and public institutions . . . abridging students' constitutional rights."[87] The ACLU puts legal muscle behind Planned Parenthood's radical agenda. Their national campaign, "Take Issue, Take Charge," lobbies to abolish abstinence education and promote comprehensive sex education in every state. Their efforts have been quite successful: The government spends $12 on comprehensive sex education to every $1 spent on abstinence education,[88] and more than half of the states have rejected over $50 million in federal grant money for abstinence education.

Comprehensive sex education programs are sometimes veiled under terms such as abstinence "plus" or abstinence "based" in order to make them appear as if they promote chastity. However, within these programs, abstinence is often presented as merely a way to prevent pregnancy and STDs. It isn't considered virtuous, nor is it seen as an expected standard of behavior for teens. It's simply one option among others. Meanwhile, these programs are adamant in promoting the idea that "unprotected sex" is irresponsible, while "protected sex" is commonplace, responsible, natural, and even fulfilling.

These programs have virtually nothing to say about the problems of casual sex, the merits of abstinence, or the connection of sex to marriage, intimacy, relationships, and emotional health (none of which is inherently "religious" content, despite the claims of the opposition). Such curricula might claim to be "morally neutral," but the crucial content they omit makes them about as neutral as hedonism and relativism. As would be expected, recent polls show that "less than 10 percent of parents support the main values and messages of comprehensive sex education programs."[89]

Therefore, every responsible parent must protect his children from the radical promiscuity agenda that has made its way into countless classrooms. Beware of anything entitled "sex education," "abstinence plus (or based) education," "family life classes," or even "health classes." And if Planned Parenthood is active in your child's school, you can be assured that what you're teaching your child at home about sex, love, and family life is being systematically deconstructed.

It is important to note that you even need to be vigilant at trustworthy public schools where your child might be taught the biology of sex in a way that is "morally neutral." Teens should not be given a biological presentation about sex with no mention of its moral implications. This ends up being far from morally neutral, despite the good intentions of your child's science or health teacher. It inadvertently promotes the philosophy that sex is void of any higher meaning. "For this reason," John Paul II said, "the Church is firmly opposed to an often widespread form of imparting sex information dissociated from moral principles."[90] Sex is too profound a topic, too wrought with implications, and too integral to who we are as human beings to be taught merely as a matter of biology. It always needs to be presented together with moral formation, within the context of the vocation to love.

Abstinence under attack in the media

Despite the fact that numerous scientific studies have proven that teens benefit from abstinence education and abstinence pledges, such studies receive little publicity.[91] The only time abstinence education seems to make headlines is when its effectiveness is called into question.

One example among many occurred when a study was published in the January 2009 edition of the journal *Pediatrics*.[92] In it, a scientist from Johns Hopkins University compared a group of teens who had made abstinence pledges with a group of teens who had not. She concluded that there was little difference between the sexual behaviors of the two, seeming to prove that virginity pledges—and through guilt by association, abstinence education—are ineffective.

Media outlets jumped on the story, each regurgitating it in their own way. "Virginity Pledges Don't Stop Teen Sex," said CBS News. "Virginity pledges don't mean much," CNN added. "Study questions virginity pledges," the *Chicago Tribune* trumpeted. Millions of Americans read the headlines, and were left to assume that abstinence education is pointless and futile.

However, the author of the study wasn't comparing teens who received abstinence education with those who didn't. A closer look at the original study shows that the research compared teens who were raised in conservative, religious households who signed virginity pledges with teens from the same background who didn't sign such pledges. The only thing proven by the study was that the sexual activity rate of deeply religious teens does not change depending upon whether or not they signed virginity pledges. If a teen is raised in a conservative family environment—and were most likely taught chastity at home and at church—it makes little difference whether or not they physically signed a pledge card. Pledge or no pledge, they're still more likely to be chaste than the average teen! Unfortunately, the correct explanation of the research received almost no attention.[93]

Such instances of the media distorting abstinence studies have been commonplace, especially when Congress is about to vote on whether or not to fund abstinence education in schools. In one such case, Mathematica Policy Research, Inc. announced that abstinence education had no impact on the sexual behavior of students. Their findings were broadcast throughout the media, and were even used as evidence on Capitol Hill to testify against federal funding for abstinence.

However, those who used this as evidence against teaching teens about abstinence might be surprised to learn that no teenagers were included in the six-million-dollar study! The subjects of the research were between the ages of 9 and 11—which is hardly the age at which young people understand the relevance of an abstinence message. The study had no high school component, and the students had no follow-up to the program, especially when they would have needed it the most, during the teenage years. In the words of the Mathematica researchers, "The findings provide no information on the effects programs might have if they were implemented for high school youth or began at earlier ages but continued to serve youth through high school."[94] However, this minor detail didn't stop ABC News from printing the headline: "'Abstinence Only' Sex Ed Ineffective."[95]

Abstinence undermined by "health-care" professionals

The radical promiscuity agenda also has the support of countless health-care professionals. They can be found working in school nurse offices, at family practices, and even at the NIH (National Institutes of Health—the primary federal agency for conducting and supporting medical research). Shockingly, the law sometimes gives them access to your child's sexual life that you might not have.

Parental consent is required to give a minor aspirin at school—yet many school nurses can hand out condoms without parental approval. Planned Parenthood clinics can provide abortions and birth control pills to 12-year-old girls without their parents finding out![96] Planned Parenthood's Web site even gives advice to minors who want an abortion but feel that they "can't tell a parent," including advice on how to have a "bypass procedure" in the states requiring parental consent or notification for abortion, enabling them to "bypass" mom and dad legally.[97]

However, the corruption extends far beyond the walls of Planned Parenthood. In September 2009, newspapers across the country announced that the government was fining Pfizer Pharmaceuticals a record $2.3 billion for illegal drug promotions. In the drug industry, companies hire pharmaceutical sales representatives to pitch their products to doctors. Normally, the business meetings take place in the doctor's office. However, Pfizer reps have been caught wining and dining the doctors. In an effort to butter up the doctors to carry their drugs (including the dangerous birth-control injection Depo Provera), Pfizer sales reps were caught paying for golf, massages, and resort junkets.[98] Thankfully, the government caught Pfizer in the act (for the fourth time in the past decade), and will now be monitoring their marketing strategies.

It's one thing to distrust Planned Parenthood and the mainstream media, but when a parent needs to question their own pediatrician and principal, you know that the culture is in need of serious intervention.

What's a parent to do?

Despite all of the forces that seek to undermine your efforts to raise chaste teens, there is much you can do to protect your family. In terms of sex education in schools, public schools are typically respectful of a parent's religious beliefs. They don't have much of a choice in this regard because of the litigious nature of our society.

Therefore, ask to review the curriculum and *all* materials used, including books, recommended Web sites, videos, etc. Make sure they match the values you teach your child at home. You might end up happily surprised, since some schools have excellent abstinence education programs. If the school's program does not meet your expectations, do not hesitate to pull your child out of class. Never let a school tell you that this is not an option. Meanwhile, you may want to consider sending your child to a private school, if possible. Research shows that "youth attending parochial schools, which tend to have more conservative values regarding sex outside of marriage, are less likely to initiate sex than those attending public schools."[99]

However, if you keep your child in a public-school setting, it isn't enough to oppose their program and flee from the curriculum. Be proactive, and seek to replace it with something that will benefit all of the students. Do some research and meet with the principal, health teacher, or school board, and propose an alternative curriculum. (See the resource section for organizations that will help you do this.) If the school's choice of curriculum is determined by the school district, go to them and work to make a positive change. Who knows? You might be surprised by the response of the administration. Many times they are on the fence, wanting to do the right thing, and needing nothing more than a nudge in the right direction and the resources to make it happen. Plenty of research has been conducted to prove the effectiveness of abstinence education, so make sure to supply them with the evidence. (See the research library at chastity. com for more on this.)

It helps to find other like-minded parents to join your crusade. Although many parents don't get involved, 91 percent think teens should abstain from sexual activity at least through high school. Comprehensive sex-education classes typically teach that sexual activity in high school is acceptable, as long as a condom is used. However, a mere 7 percent of parents agree with this message.[100] It usually only takes one person to inspire other parents to work for change. Although few want to lead, many will follow a leader with whom they agree.

Most parents certainly don't want teachers filling their children's minds with explicit sexual images between math and history classes. They don't want their children practicing condom use on bananas in the classroom.[101] And they don't want their kindergartners taught why it's "normal" for a man to marry another man (as is happening in states that have legalized same-sex marriage). But all that means very little because most parents fail to ask questions, fail to protest, and fail to opt out. As Edmund Burke is famously credited with saying, "All that is necessary for the triumph of evil is that good men do nothing." Therefore, don't be afraid to act. It might cost you some popularity with the school board, your peers, or even your own child, but it's worth it.

GROUP STUDY QUESTIONS:

1. What shocked you the most from this chapter?
2. What kind of sex education did you receive in school?
3. Do you know what is being taught in your child's school regarding the topic of sexuality? What will you do to find out?
4. Since so many parents oppose the message of comprehensive sex education, why do you think so few of them protest it in their schools?
5. In what ways can you help your local school(s) to promote the message of purity to teens in your community?

6.

Set the standard high and clear.

"Do not be conformed to this world but be transformed by the renewal of your mind, that you may prove what is the will of God, what is good and acceptable and perfect."
(Rom 12:2)

"Don't flutter about like a hen, when you can soar to the heights of an eagle."
—St. Josemaria Escriva

Because teenagers require concrete guidelines, parents need to set the standard high and describe it clearly when it comes to premarital sexual activity. If the call to be *abstinent* sets the standard high, expecting abstinence *until marriage* makes the standard clear. All too often, parents slip into the habit of encouraging abstinence "until later," "until you're more mature," or "until you're ready." However, these guidelines are vague. Telling a teen not to do something until he is more mature is giving him a green light. I don't know about you, but when I was 15, I had never been so mature in my entire life! However, when you tell teens that they should abstain until after their wedding, there is no doubt as to how you expect them to behave in the meantime.

Some parents, with the best of intentions, set the bar low. They point out the ideal path for their child (abstinence), but add the caveat, "but I know you're a teen, and you're probably going to end up doing it anyway. So, just make sure to use protection." Contrary to what many may believe, these parents are *not* sending a mixed message. They're sending a very clear one: I expect you to fail.

Curiously, such parents would never tell their children, "Don't drink and drive. But if you do, make sure to drive in the slow lane." Or, "I don't want you to smoke, but I'm going to give you this package of low-tar cigarettes, in case you're going to do it anyway." Yet when it comes to sexual activity, they lower their expectations. Not surprisingly, a study of 10 thousand teenagers showed that teens who believe their mothers approve of birth control are twice as likely to engage in sex.[102] This correlation can be caused by a number of factors, but it should not come as a surprise. The National Campaign to Prevent Teen Pregnancy surveyed teenagers about this and asked, "Suppose a parent or other adult tells you/a teen the following: 'Don't have sex, but if you do you should use birth control or protection.' Do you think this is a message that encourages you/ teens to have sex?" Nearly half of the teens answered "Yes."[103] This is obviously a dangerous message because those who believe in the concept of "safe sex" engage in what scientists call "behavioral disinhibition." In other words, they often engage in risky behavior because they have a false sense of security.[104]

Thankfully, the Catholic Church has spoken clearly against the false notion of safe sex: "This position [safe sex], in itself contrary to morality, also turns out to be fallacious and ends up increasing promiscuity and free sexual activity through a false idea of safety. Objective and scientifically rigorous studies have shown the high percentage of the failure of these means."[105]

Safe sex and STDs

Teens often think that a condom will provide them with 99 percent protection from STDs, but such a statistic is far from reality. According to the National Institutes of Health, a condom will reduce the risk of HIV transmission by only 85 percent.[106] As for the other STDs, the available scientific evidence suggests that the condom reduces STD transmission only by about half.[107]

The most common STD, Human Papillomavirus (HPV), can lead to cervical cancer as well as genital warts. Because of its link to cervical cancer, HPV kills more American women than HIV. However, the condom only offers minimal protection from the virus because it is spread from skin-to-skin contact throughout the entire genital area, including thighs and lower abdomen.[108] How big is the problem? The Centers for Disease Control reported that *the majority of sexually active women have been infected with one or more types of genital HPV.*[109]

Vaccines have been created to deal with this epidemic, and can greatly reduce the risk of cervical cancer and genital warts caused by HPV. Although the vaccines prevent the two strains of the virus that are responsible for causing 70 percent of cervical cancer, they offer no protection from the other cancer-causing HPV types. Therefore, a significant cancer risk still remains for vaccinated girls. Furthermore, the injections are not without their own side-effects. Regarding the vaccination of their children, parents should research the issue thoroughly rather than leaving the decision to their pediatrician. Check out the research library at chastityproject.com for information regarding HPV vaccines.

The fact that condoms do not offer sufficient protection against disease has been illustrated on the global canvas time and again. In the African nations Botswana, Cameroon, and Kenya—which all have aggressive condom distribution programs—HIV increased alongside condom distribution. In Cameroon, condom sales increased from six million to 15 million in a span of less than 10 years. During the same time, HIV rates tripled! The journal *Studies in Family Planning* pointed this out in their article "Condom Promotion for AIDS Prevention in the Developing World: Is It Working?" Its authors noted that "high HIV transmission rates have continued despite high rates of condom use. . . . *No clear examples have emerged yet of a country that has turned back a generalized epidemic primarily by means of condom promotion.*"[110]

Conversely, in predominantly Catholic Uganda, condoms did not enter the scene until 1995 and are promoted as a last resort, while abstinence initiatives are well-funded and take center stage. When compared with other African nations, Uganda has been uniquely successful. According to the BBC News, "Uganda has performed well in bringing down the HIV prevalence to around 6 percent. In many parts of the country, it was at least three times as high during the early 1990s."[111] The *Journal of International Development* noted that it was "the *lack* of condom promotion during the 1980s and early 1990s [that] contributed to the relative success of behavior change strategies in Uganda."[112]

The ineffectiveness of condoms is also illustrated in Asia. The Philippines and Thailand reported their first case of HIV in 1984. The Philippines, an overwhelmingly Catholic nation, promoted abstinence. Thailand was flooded with condoms. Over 20 years later the rate of HIV in Thailand is 50 times that of the Philippines.[113] While some people see the Catholic Church as an obstacle to STD prevention, the *British Medical Journal* noted, "The greater the percentage of Catholics in any country, the lower the level of HIV. If the Catholic Church is promoting a message about HIV in those countries, it seems to be working."[114]

One final reason why the "safe sex" message has failed to curb the STD epidemic is that the "protection" offered by the condom decreases with repeated exposures.[115] Even an 85 percent risk reduction doesn't add up to much when the risks are taken repeatedly. In Africa, one Harvard researcher noted, "20 years into the pandemic there is no evidence that more condoms leads to less AIDS. . . . Over a lifetime, it is the number of sexual partners [that matter]. *Condom levels are found to be non-determining of HIV infection levels.*"[116]

"Safe sex" didn't work for Thailand or Cameroon and it certainly isn't working in the U.S. where more than 52 thousand people will get an STD today, almost half of them under the age of 24.[117] The calculus of condoms is simple. Decrease the risk a little, increase the number of risk-takers, and the end result is far worse than before "protection" was available.

Safe sex and pregnancy

If condoms have failed to stem the tide of the STD epidemic, it's no surprise that they have proved inadequate in reducing teen pregnancy rates. According to the research institute of Planned Parenthood, the condom failure rate in preventing pregnancy is 15 percent during the first year of use.[118] Some might assume that hormonal birth control would be far more effective, but for the first year of use for women under the age of 20, the pill has an annual failure rate of 8 to 13 percent.[119] That's why even Planned Parenthood's research institute had to admit that most high school pregnancies are caused by contraceptive failure, not by the failure to use them.[120]

Nonetheless, many parents have turned to hormonal contraceptives like pills or Depo Provera (the shot) to protect their daughters from an untimely pregnancy. In their zeal to prevent pregnancy, most of these parents fail to evaluate the dangers of these methods.

For example, birth-control pills interfere with a woman's immune system,[121] making her more likely to contract certain STDs.[122] Among countless other side effects, the pill increases a woman's chance of having breast cancer,[123] cervical cancer,[124] liver cancer,[125] and potentially fatal blood clots.[126] The pill can also permanently decrease a woman's libido,[127] and Depo Provera is so effective in producing the same effect that some states mandate it as a punishment for male sex offenders![128] However, because of its link to breast cancer, veterinarians stopped prescribing Depo-Provera for dogs.[129] The litany of potential side-effects is so long that any parent who wishes to protect a daughter should think twice about temporarily sterilizing her through hormone manipulation.

Even if there were a way to protect a child's body from all the effects of sexual activity, the person would still not be protected from the emotional and spiritual damage that takes place. For this reason, some might argue that the very notion of safe sex is degrading; it reduces a person to his or her genitals. In other words, as long as a woman doesn't get pregnant or infected, she's safe! What about the rest of the human person?

Unfortunately, because the world does not believe in the power of young people to do the right thing, teens rarely hear about the benefits of purity. For example, the average sex-ed class spends less than

5 percent of class time talking to teens about abstinence, with much of the remaining 95 percent of the
time heavily focused on contraception.[130] This sends
a clear message to teens: "We don't believe you have
the power to abstain." When teens are told they can't
control themselves, it becomes a self-fulfilling proph-
ecy. A generation of teens has been living down to the
expectations of the "sex-perts."

Called to greatness

We need to remember that young people are capable
of greatness. Some of the greatest saints and heroes in
the history of the Church were teens. One is Bl. José
Sanchez del Río. José was martyred during the persecu-
tion of Catholics that occurred in the early part of the
20th century in Mexico. He joined a Catholic group
knowing that he was putting his life at risk. When the
authorities caught him, they put him in jail. His ticket
to freedom was to renounce his Catholic faith.

To scare him into submission, they forced him to
witness the hanging of another Catholic. Instead, he
encouraged his fellow inmate saying, "You will be in
heaven before me. Prepare a place for me. Tell Christ
the King I shall be with him soon."

José's father tried to ransom his son's life but raised
the money too late. When his time came, soldiers
shaved off the soles of his feet and made him walk on

salt, and then through the dusty streets of his town. Time and again they offered him freedom and a safe return to his parents if only he would say "Death to Christ the King." Groaning in pain, he refused their offer, shouting, "Long live Christ the King! Long live Our Lady of Guadalupe!" When they taunted him and asked what they should tell his parents, he replied that they would see each other in heaven. They walked him to the cemetery, pointed their guns at him, and offered him freedom one last time. "Long live Christ the King!" he shouted again.[131] The soldiers bayoneted him. Before a final gunshot ended his life, he drew a cross in the dirt with his own blood and kissed it. Bl. José was only 14.

While there are few, if any, perfect teens (or parents for that matter), all teens are capable of heroism once they grasp that something is worth being heroic about. They are certainly ready for heroic love. Teens want authentic love. They want to be told that they are capable of attaining a love that is beautiful, noble, good, and true. But the world expects so little of them. It's no wonder so many teens see traditional Christianity as boring and prudish. Mediocrity has no allure. Perhaps that's why millions of young people flocked to World Youth Days to see John Paul II, who encouraged them to become the "saints of the new millennium." He was over 80 years old and crippled by Parkinson's, but he could draw more teens than any rock band could ever hope to!

Within each young person there is a Bl. José waiting to happen, if only there were more adults expecting it. Your voice needs to be loud and clear, and in stark contrast with a world that is leading teens into disaster with its low expectations of them. Let them know that purity is possible, that you expect greatness from them, and that you believe in them. If you do, they'll be more likely to expect greatness from themselves.

GROUP STUDY QUESTIONS:

1. Why do you think the dangers of "safe sex" are so rarely publicized?
2. Have you ever explained to your teen why "safe sex" is unsafe?
3. Why do you feel it's important not to waver when delivering the message of chastity for teens?
4. If abstinence education has been so successful in preventing the spread of HIV in certain areas of the world, why do you think it receives so little recognition?
5. Why do you think so many adults have such low expectations of teenagers? How do you think this has impacted teens today?

7.

Protect your teen from the media.

"No temptation has overtaken you that is not common to man. God is faithful, and he will not let you be tempted beyond your strength, but with the temptation will also provide the way of escape, that you may be able to endure it."
(1 Cor 10:13)

"The devil is like a rabid dog tied to a chain; beyond the length of the chain he cannot seize anyone. And you: Keep at a distance. If you approach too near, you let yourself be caught. Remember that the devil has only one door by which to enter the soul: the will."
—St. Padre Pio

Media Saturation

The average American youth spends more than 7½ hours per day with various forms of media (television, music, video games, Internet, etc.). If you account for the time they spend multitasking (using more than one form of media at a time), they pack in a total of nearly 11 hours per day![132] And this does not even include the 2½ hours young cell phone users spend texting and talking each day! Without question, young people spend more time engaged in these activities than any other, including sleep or school. Today, it seems like the only way to get your child's attention would be to get your own TV show (not that he'd watch).

Fifty years ago, consuming so much media content would have been more a waste of time than a danger to the soul. After all, television sitcoms such as *I Love Lucy* depicted married couples sleeping in separate beds. Nowadays, the sitcoms portray single parents raising teens while the unmarried teens are sharing beds with each other. In fact, of the television programming most frequently watched by adolescents, 82 percent contains some sexual content.[133] Yet only 10 percent of these shows include some mention of risk or responsibilities associated with sex.[134]

While many have argued that such entertainment is harmless, the medical journal *Pediatrics* stated that teens who are exposed to more sexual content in the media are more likely to initiate early sexual activity and become pregnant.[135] According to research on more than 1,700 teens, "youths who watched the most sexual content 'acted older': a 12-year-old at the highest levels of exposure behaved like a 14- or 15-year-old at the lowest levels."[136] Without question, teens who ingest massive amounts of sexual content on TV develop more sex-saturated thinking patterns, and they tend to live accordingly.

Unfortunately, the TV is practically given the position of a shrine in most homes. Not only does it have primacy in its location, 8 of 10 teens report that their family leaves the TV on "some" or "most" of the time throughout the day, even if nobody is watching it! Even during meals, nearly two-thirds of teens report that the TV usually remains on.[137] Seventy-one percent of teens have a TV in the bedroom, too. Teens with a TV in the bedroom spend nearly 400 hours more per year sitting in front of a screen![138] Granted, it's easier to refuse to give your child a TV than it is to remove one once you've allowed it. Pulling a TV out of your teen's room may be about as easy as pulling out her wisdom teeth without anesthesia. But perhaps it's time.

But TV is just the beginning. When a teen leaves the house, he often watches movies in the car or on his MP3 player. Or he might visit a friend's house to play video games. Those who play video games typically spend about

14 hours per week engaged in the activity.[139] The net effect of all this noise is that young people become bored, impatient, and more disconnected from their families.

Surprisingly, the largest consumers of the media are not older teens, but rather 11- to 14-year-olds.[140] As they transition into adolescence, their media use explodes. For this reason, parents must take measures to restrict not only the *quality* of media which a young person receives, but also the *quantity*. Give a teen his own video-game system, Internet access, iPod, cell phone, laptop, and TV, and you're probably not going to see him until he emerges from his room just in time to leave for college. Rules need to be established. In fact, teens whose parents don't set rules on media usage typically spend about three hours more per day with it.[141]

Through the media, today's youth are inundated with an IV drip of lust and instant gratification. Hollywood and MTV are not merely stealing your children's time, but are using that time to offer them a twisted form of sex "education." Do you feel prepared to decline the offer and protect your children? Parents must make themselves aware of where the dangers lurk, specifically through the Internet and cell phones.

Internet

While the Internet can be a great tool for research and social networking, it also poses a grave and imminent moral danger to your family. Consider the following:

- To stir up business for the adult entertainment industry, approximately 2.5 billion pornographic e-mails are sent each day.[142]
- The Internet hosts more than four million pornographic Web sites, containing 420 million pages of images and videos.[143]
- In an effort to hook children on porn, adult entertainment companies have purchased dozens of Web site domain names that belong to children's toys and have used them for pornography.
- Ninety percent of 8- to 16-year-olds have viewed porn online (most while doing homework).[144]

Unless you are protecting your children from Internet pornography, they are almost certainly going to be exposed to it. Therefore, parents need to become computer-literate and take measures to secure the family computer(s). Here's how:

1. Make the computer more public. Put it in a high-traffic area of your house with the monitor easily visible to others. Do not give your teen Internet access in his bedroom.
2. Learn to check the history files on your computer. On a PC, open your Internet browser, click "tools,"

then "Internet options," then "settings," then "view files." That will bring up a list of all Web sites that have been visited on your computer. A clever teen might cover his tracks by deleting these files. To prevent this, lock the history files so that they cannot be deleted without a password. You can also install a piece of equipment known as a "keyboard logger" that can record the last million or more keystrokes on your computer, allowing you to keep track of any inappropriate Web sites, e-mails, or chat room discussions.

3. Put a filter on your computer to block out impure Web sites. Start by opening your Internet browser, click "tools," then "Internet options," then "content," then "enable." This will allow you to filter out many inappropriate Web sites. However, it is recommended that you take advantage of some of the more advanced forms of Internet safety. To do this, see our recommended sites in the resource section at the back of this booklet.

4. Be aware that pornography is not simply on XXX Web sites. For example, one of the most popular Web sites for teens is YouTube. Despite their efforts to block users from uploading porn videos, YouTube is littered with them.

5. If a member of your family views pornography, talk to him about it. Make use of some of the Web sites

and products in the resource section to help him break free from it.

6. If your teen uses social networking sites, such as MySpace or Facebook, make sure his profile is set to private. That way, your teen will be less likely to receive sexual solicitations from strangers.

7. Be on guard with regards to the use of instant messaging. Chat rooms are a common place for sexual predators to seek out victims. It is important that your child be educated (at the appropriate time) on the reality of sexual predators and how they operate. Sex offenders will often pose as teens, seeking private information from your children such as their home address, pictures, and the time they leave school. Teach your children never to give out such information online.

8. If you have a founded suspicion that your teens may be harming themselves or others, you have the ability (and the right) to monitor their e-mail and text messages. Some computer software enables you to receive notices when your child is sending inappropriate text messages or e-mail. You can also receive copies of their e-mail, and sometimes retrieve deleted text messages. Details on these programs can be found in the resource section at the back of this book. Obviously, such drastic surveillance measures should only be used for serious reasons. However, a

teen should know that they do not possess an absolute right to privacy. How do you know when to snoop? Trust them until you have a reason not to.

9. Be aware of what kinds of video games are being played in your house. In 2005, a video game entitled *Grand Theft Auto* made headlines when it was discovered that users could download codes from the Internet to unlock secret sex scenes. The same video game also allows the players to visit strip clubs, engage in prostitution, steal cars, and murder police officers. As if that weren't heinous enough, the game enables users to keep track of how much money they have spent on prostitutes and gives them the option of murdering or beating the prostitute in order to reclaim the money given to her. When young people were surveyed about their media consumption, 72 percent of the 15- to 18-year-olds had played *Grand Theft Auto*, as had 25 percent of 8- to 10-year-olds![145] Considering there are thousands of video games available, it is essential that parents look closely at the rating on each video game *and* research it prior to making a purchase for their teen. Many of the games rated for teens depict women in degrading ways, so do not be fooled by a label.

10. While teens still purchase music CDs, a far more common source for music is the Internet. Instead of spending $20 on a CD, a teen can simply download

favorite tunes online. At least with a CD, the concerned parent can read the lyrics in order to decide if the content is appropriate. However, with today's digital music collections, parents need to do more homework. If you want to know the lyrics of a song, simply do an Internet search. Type in the name of the song and add the word "lyrics." You'll find Web sites that provide the lyrics from any artist. Also, take advantage of resources such as Focus on the Family's Web site "pluggedin.com." This site allows parents to easily search through hundreds of music reviews. Parents can also access reviews of video games, television shows, and movies, while learning about positive alternatives. Considering that the average 15- to 18-year-old spends more than three hours per day listening to music, you can't afford to be unplugged.[146]

Sexting

Twenty-two percent of teenage girls admit to electronically sending or posting online nude or semi-nude pictures of themselves. Thirty-seven percent of teenage girls have sent sexually suggestive messages through e-mail, text, or instant messaging (IM). While boys are less likely to send pictures of themselves, they're more likely to send sexual messages and request photos. Overall, 48 percent of teens admit to having received a sexual message through text, e-mail, or IM.[147] Considering that the average teen who texts sends more than 100 text messages a day,[148] it's hard to imagine that they haven't all received an inappropriate one by now.

What can you do as a parent to protect your teenage boy or girl from sexual solicitations? The first step is to consider whether or not your child needs a cell phone. Many educators have pointed out that cell phones allow teens to circumvent parents as their gatekeepers. Years ago, if a boy called a young woman, her parents would answer the phone and screen the call: "And whom may I say is calling?" Now, girls can stay up until two o'clock in the morning, secretly texting a boy from their bedroom. If you feel that your child needs a cell phone, at least give the device a curfew!

Another step to take is to warn them against sending such messages. Remind them that any pictures they send of themselves can never be retrieved. Although they might assume the message was sent privately, it becomes public property as soon as they click "send" and can remain in cyberspace indefinitely. This means that if a girl sends a provocative photo to her boyfriend and the relationship later turns sour, the image can easily find its way to the Internet or be forwarded to other cell phones throughout school. Aside from the immediate embarrassment this may cause, it can also have enduring effects. When she applies for a job years later, an employer might pull up the image while doing a background check.

Aside from the nuisance of having incriminating photographs permanently in circulation, the practice itself is illegal. If high school students are sending—or even receiving—sexual images of classmates electronically, they can be indicted for distributing or possessing child pornography. Being found guilty of child porn charges does not look impressive on a job resume.

If you have a reason to suspect that your teens are defying your wishes to keep their texting clean, you can install software to monitor the messaging. (See the resource section.) If a teen is aware that his parent has such capabilities, he's less likely to engage in risqué chats and image-sending.

GROUP STUDY QUESTIONS:

1. How has your home been infiltrated by bad media?
2. What rules have you established in your home to protect the innocence of your family from the media? Have you set boundaries for time as well as content?
3. Do you feel that you have a good grasp of how to protect your children from the various ways that their purity is threatened through today's technology? (And are you sure your Internet blocks are effective enough?)
4. When inappropriate content is shown on your television while your children are watching, what do you do?
5. How will your child respond to blocks and monitors on his media? Will that affect your decision to monitor him?

8.

Delay the onset of dating.

"Do not arouse, do not stir up love, before its own
time."
(Song 8:4 *NAB*)

"Now is the time to begin to prepare yourself for
family life. You cannot fulfill this path if you do not
know how to love. To love means to want to perfect
yourself and your beloved, to overcome your
selfishness, and give yourself completely."[149]
—St. Gianna Beretta Molla

It is up to you, as the parent, to determine an appropriate dating age. The Church does not propose a specific age. After all, some teens might be mature enough to date, while some 35-year-olds are not. That said, we strongly recommend a "no dating" policy at least until your child is 16, preferably older, and with plenty of adult supervision. Given their level of emotional and neurological development, dating before 16 can lead to unnecessary pain and confusion in your child's life. Consider that the DMV will not even entrust your child with a car before that age, and your child is of far greater value (and more difficult to fix) than your Honda.

At first, your teen might balk at this idea because of the enormous pressure they may feel to find a boyfriend or girlfriend as early as elementary school. But perhaps it will take some of the social pressure off your child if you suggest that she simply blame you to her friends and would-be boyfriends. After witnessing the emotional turmoil that accompanies typical high school relationships, many teens later express gratitude to their parents for helping to spare them from needless drama. In the words of one young woman who e-mailed us,

> I'm almost 16 years old and a sophomore in high school, but I've never had a boyfriend. At first this was because I'm not

allowed to date until I'm 16 (one of the best decisions my parents ever made, especially because they gave me reasons even when I was really young), but now it's also because I haven't met anyone who I really want to be with. It's taught me to notice more about a guy than his appearance or reputation; I find myself looking much more at personality.

It's important that parents not only delay the age at which their children may date, but that they also teach them the purpose of dating, the dangers of dating too early, and offer an alternative vision for young romance. Here are some points you can share with your child about why you would like them to delay dating:

1. *Dating is for discerning marriage.* Simply put, the purpose of dating is to find a spouse. Given this fact, there isn't much sense in dating during the high school years. This does not mean barring dances, group dating, or friendships with members of the opposite sex. Rather, it means that committed, romantic relationships should be entered into when marriage is reasonably within reach.

   When a society loses sight of the purpose of dating, dating ends up accomplishing the opposite of its purpose. Instead of preparing them for marriage, it teaches young people how to break up. A person who dates successfully breaks up with everyone in his life except for one person. While this is great preparation for divorce, it is not good preparation for a successful marriage.

While the majority of relationships do not end in marriage, some become so intimate and intense that the couple seems emotionally married. If a break-up occurs, they experience a sort of emotional divorce. It is not uncommon that by the time a person is married, he feels as if he has already been divorced several times. After a relationship ends, a teen often thinks, "I never should have dated that person in the first place!" But how many teens pause to ask themselves before a relationship begins, "Can I see myself marrying this person?" If the answer is unclear, it's all the more reason to take your time.

If your teen struggles to understand this, say: "Let's imagine you meet a boy or girl you would love to marry, but marriage is still a decade away. What do you think would be more likely to last 10 years: a high-school relationship or a solid friendship? The friendship is more easily maintained and will serve as a foundation for any lasting love that does unfold. Besides, what is the point of committing to someone when you know you're probably going to break up when you go to college in two years? What many people do not realize is that you don't need to date in high school to get to know the opposite sex or to have a successful relationship in college. Do not worry that you will never find love if you do not rush into romance now. Take this time to be free from distractions and ask yourself what God wants of you during these years. Unreservedly give your youth to him, and watch what he will do in your life."

2. *Early dating puts purity at risk.* A study of over 800 high school students was conducted to determine how their dating age affected their sexual behavior. Here's what the researchers found: Among teens who began dating in seventh grade, only 29 percent of boys and 10 percent of girls were still virgins. However, of those who waited until they were 16 to date, 84 percent of boys and 82 percent of girls were still virgins.[150]

This does not mean that your children will inevitably be promiscuous if they start dating when they are 12, but the increased risk is obvious.

3. *High school is the time for discovering who you are; intense dating can hinder that process.* According to Erik Erikson's theory of psychosocial development, adolescence is a key time of identity formation when

young people explore who they are, how they are perceived by others, and where their lives are going.

Your child's most profound identity is as a beloved son or daughter of God. They need to be taught this reality from childhood. It forms the most stable foundation for self-worth, purpose, and security that a person can have. But there are many other ways your child will still need to discover who he is as he becomes an adult.

Forming self-perception can be a difficult and bewildering experience. Instead of exploring and forming their own identity, many teens begin looking for a sense of security in another person. They don't feel complete unless they are paired up with someone else and frantically search for their self-worth and their identity in a relationship.

It is crucial that young people not perceive themselves as incomplete without a boyfriend or girlfriend. If they do, it will be difficult for them to experience truly healthy and self-giving relationships. Instead, relationships will be sought out of desperation for security and self-worth, often even into adulthood. They will be willing to compromise their deepest values and beliefs in order to be with someone.

Point out to your child what is going on in her heart. Teens might attempt to find their identity and worth in many silly ways, but once they realize what they are doing, they often reconsider. Let your child know that even though many girls look for their self-worth in boys, a girl should never allow her value to be determined by what a boy thinks of her. (Remember, you are setting the bar high.) High school is not the time for her to be consumed by relationships. It is a time to solidify her identity, identify her dreams, discover the world, and set the course for life. It is a time for enjoying family, forming deep friendships, developing gifts, embarking on adventures, growing in faith, and experiencing the difference you can make in the world. It's also a time when it's natural to experience intense feelings for a member of the opposite sex. But there's no need to complicate those feelings by dating—which imposes everyone else's expectations on a couple.

4. *Dating often ruins what might have otherwise blossomed into mature romance.* It's normal to have intense feelings for someone during the teenage years. Those feelings can be even more intense than in adulthood because of the lack of rational thought accompanying them. Brushing aside your child's feelings will only lead to them keeping those feelings secret from you. Always take your child seriously. Keep in mind that it *is* possible (though rare) for someone to marry a high school sweetheart. Talk to your children about their

crushes, but also direct them. While crushes can lead to special friendships, they should not always lead to dating. After all, such friendships have far more potential to last through college than high-school flings.

Ask your teen questions such as: "When you look at dating relationships at your school, what are you seeing? How long do most of these relationships last? Do many of the couples remain friends after their relationships end? Does it seem to be working?" Odds are your teen will reply that most of the relationships are short-lived and filled with drama. Once the relationship fizzles, the couples are often bitter and alienated from one another. Sometimes lasting friendships are also sacrificed for the sake of a dating relationship that does not last. Although it is unfortunate to see, the confusion and disorder of most teenage relationships will add weight to your case. You could also ask, "Why do you think most of these relationships crumble? If everyone is looking for love, why does it seem so hard to find?"

The answer is simple: Because of bad timing and a lack of direction, dating has spoiled many potentially good relationships. Rather than allowing a relationship to unfold naturally, the modern concept of dating urges teens to allow emotions and infatuation to dictate the course of a relationship. We're not proposing that all crushes be "crushed," but that young people learn from past generations about how romance should blossom.

Learning from the past

In past generations, dating was done with a purpose. People didn't make their hearts and lives vulnerable to one another for fun, but to discern marriage. This was not a private affair, but something that involved the input of others. Such involvement helped a couple to discern with a clear mind and a pure heart. This traditional form of dating was called "courtship."

The modern idea of dating is only about a century old. Originally, the purpose of dating and courtship was to find a husband or wife. If a man wished to enjoy the company of a woman, he would do so in the presence of her family, with the intention of perhaps winning her hand in marriage. Gradually, this focus was lost as young men and women moved the setting of a relationship away from the context of the family to a more private location. With this loss of connection to the family came a loss of guidance and purpose in relationships. Many people began to date for the sake of dating, as opposed to dating for the sake of finding a spouse. Because so many couples today lack a sense of direction, more relationships than ever are heading nowhere. In order to prevent your children from experiencing the heartbreak of pointless relationships, introduce them to the wisdom of the past.

For teens, the term "courtship" will be foreign. They might wonder if you're hoping to arrange their marriage, so it's not necessary to use the term. Just introduce them to the concept of traditional romance. Once they see the logic of courtship, they'll be more likely to take it seriously. Let them know that your goal is not to rob them of freedom, but to help them to find the love they deserve.

When your child is mature enough to date, teaching her the principles of courtship will give her greater confidence in relationships. Here are four basic things teens can learn from traditional courtship to help form healthy dating relationships today:

1. *Be wise about the timing and purpose of your relationship.* As we said above, the purpose of dating is to discern marriage. Given this fact, relationships, especially in high school, should be entered into slowly.

   Many relationships are rushed into, motivated by emotional needs or mere physical attraction. They lack a solid foundation. They also lack clarity of purpose. Countless teens are involved in quasi-relationships: "We're kind of dating." When these arrangements are referred to as "friends with benefits," it typically involves a boy who gladly receives physical gratification at the expense of a young girl who secretly hopes the relationship will blossom into something meaningful—which it never does. Such relationships are fueled by passion as opposed to authentic love. John Paul II rightly remarked that the "fire of pleasure . . . burns quickly like a pile of withered grass."[151]

When couples do commit, they often do it so quickly that they hardly know to whom or for what reason. As time goes by and faults come to the surface, the relationship becomes rocky.

Now, invite your teen to consider a different scenario: A young couple meet and quickly develop a strong attraction to one another. The attraction was not merely physical, but also included a deep attraction to one another's personality. Instead of rushing into a romantic relationship as their friends are doing, they take their time. They get to know one another as friends—which is the foundation of any lasting love. The season of friendship serves as a test: Can their relationship grow and thrive without physical intimacy?

Such a test weeds out many potential dates who are interested in pleasure and don't have the patience for pure friendships, sparing your child the heartbreak of being used by someone she thought was a friend. The time of friendship also allows the young man and woman to see each other's qualities. This time of mutual discovery allows the couple to discern that the other person is worth committing to—not just now, but perhaps for life.

So much is said about physical boundaries that many adults fail to remind teens that emotional boundaries are also necessary. True love requires vulnerability, and so a teen must be careful about giving away his heart. Isn't it time to take love a little more seriously? It's not that we expect our teens to marry whomever they date, but that we insist that they not make a serious romantic commitment to a person they cannot see themselves marrying.

2. *Seek the direction of those who love you the most (God, family, priests, good friends, etc).* As Proverbs says, "Without counsel plans go wrong, but with many advisers they succeed" (15:22). When a person has an unhealthy habit, he often hides it from those who love him. The same tendency exists in human relationships, where a teen will pull away from loved ones when his conscience is bothered. Courtship invites couples to do the opposite: to have the humility to seek counsel from those who love them.

3. *Spend time with one another's family.* Not only does this honor the parents, it helps couples get to know the family that they may join one day. Finally—and this may be a real eye-opener—how this person

treats his family will likely be how he treats your child when the initial infatuation tapers off. For example, if a young woman is dating a guy who is disrespectful toward his mother and sisters but is a perfect gentleman around her, guess what she has to look forward to if she settles down with him. The way a couple spends their time together determines how well they ground their relationship in reality. If they spend every waking hour tucked away in private, gazing into one another's eyes, they will never learn the full truth about each other. Spending time in service, with family, and even playing sports will help reveal the other person's identity and character (or lack thereof). And when not with family, dating time should be spent in public rather than in private. The more alone time that a teenage couple spends together, the more likely they are to find themselves failing at chastity.

4. *Be practical about whom you date.* Because of social networking available through the Internet, many teens are initiating long-distance relationships. Not only are these relationships impractical, they also leave more room for delusional ideas about the potential date and can create deep emotional attachments that rarely lead to lasting love. One California teenager took her own life after

her online boyfriend broke up with her. After the suicide, investigators discovered that the boyfriend never existed, but was a prank initiated by two other young women. Avoid such tragedies by practicing restraint in terms of impractical relationships.

You might think that long-distance relationships are safe from sexual temptations, but that is not the case. Internet chats and text messages often become very sensual because the couple does not feel the inhibitions they would if they were face to face. These relationships often become so primed with emotional and sexual tension that when the couple does finally meet, the physical intimacy skyrockets.

Teens must use some practical wisdom regarding the age of potential dates. Dating older people is especially risky for young women. Here's why: 74 percent of girls who lose their virginity as teens lose it to an older guy.[152] The majority of teen pregnancies are caused by older males.[153] Older guys are also more likely to transmit sexually transmitted diseases because they are more likely to have had multiple sexual partners.[154] Lastly, girls who date guys two or more years older are six times as likely to get drunk and smoke pot.[155] Therefore, parents would be wise to set down dating rules in terms of age differences.

Needless to say, these steps are easier to explain than they are to enforce (especially if your teen is already dating). So, don't wait for the teenage years to explain the purpose of dating as well as the age requirements you have chosen. When explaining your reasons, make sure to focus on the positive elements of courtship or traditional romance more than the negatives of modern dating. If a teen is going to embrace the concept of courtship, he or she needs to understand its benefits.

If they see that these principles will help them to find lasting love, they'll be more open to the ideas. Many teens know no other option than serial dating in order to find love. When they follow this deficient model of relationships and fail to find the kind of love that lasts, they are left to wonder where they went wrong. More often than not, they conclude that *they* are the problem, when the real problem is the confused modern idea of dating. Chaste courtship, or traditional romance, is the solution. While it cannot guarantee love, it certainly prepares for it and guards against its counterfeits.

GROUP STUDY QUESTIONS:

1. How is premature dating damaging to a teen?
2. How has our modern approach to dating been damaging to society?
3. Do you think it's realistic for teens to delay dating?
4. What can you do as a parent to help your teens avoid feeling lonely when many of their peers are in dating relationships?
5. When your child does begin a dating relationship (which might not be until after high school), how can you have an active, positive roll in ensuring it is a healthy experience?

9.

Have THE talk (but make sure it's part of a lifetime of talks).

"You shall love the LORD your God with all your heart, and with all your soul, and with all your might. And these words which I command you this day shall be upon your heart; and you shall teach them diligently to your children, and shall talk of them when you sit in your house, and when you walk by the way, and when you lie down, and when you rise."
(Dt 6:5-7)

"Men must be taught to love, and to love in a noble way; they must be educated in depth in this truth, that is, in the fact that a woman is a person and not simply an object."
—Pope John Paul II

Have THE talk (but make sure it's part of a lifetime of talks)

A high-school girl from the Midwest asked her father if he could take her and her friend to a Notre Dame football game. The fathers of the two girls were friends, so they decided to make it a father-daughter weekend. Before making the trip, the two fathers conspired to use the time to talk to the girls about chastity. After the girls hopped into the car, the dads locked the doors and announced, "Girls, because we have a seven-hour drive to South Bend, we're going to talk to you about chastity." Odds are, the girls screamed and tried to crawl out the windows. But by the end of the trip, the daughters admitted they felt grateful that their dads had the guts to talk to them about the subject.

There's no easy way to broach the subject of sexuality with your teen. But there are plenty of ways to teach them over time the beauty of God's gift of sexuality. Instead of worrying about when and how to give them the dreaded "talk," look at things in a different light. Why should one conversation dominate their education in human sexuality? In no other area of life do we expect that one talk will suffice. Students are given more than a dozen years of reading, writing, and arithmetic before they leave for college. In the same way, chastity education must be an ongoing and steady process. And while you're not going to have "the talk" about what sex *is* dozens of times, that talk has to be part of a long series of talks with your child—and more, part of an open and loving relationship you've formed with your child.

While parishes and schools can support your work as a parent by teaching about chastity and abstinence in a classroom setting, the Church recognizes that the more intimate aspects of sexual information should be taught at home.[156] Because every child is unique, there can be no standard age or grade at which certain information must be given. One 11-year-old might be ready for sensitive information that would cause discomfort and distress in another. Because of this, the Church reminds parents and educators that each child is entitled to "individualized formation" in this area.[157] This fact doesn't fit well with mass education, and for that reason, when it comes to this subject, every family should regard itself as a homeschooling family.

Teaching your child about the more intimate aspects of sexuality is something you can never completely delegate to someone else. Churches and schools don't exist to replace you in your task, but to support you in it. What matters most is that you are in charge of your child's education on this delicate subject. As mentioned earlier, make sure you preview any material that will be presented to your children. Pull them out if a lesson is too explicit. Or, if you are in need of the help of a trustworthy expert to convey certain information, be present during the lesson.[158]

If the school is planning on teaching your child the birds and the bees, it's better to relieve them of this task and cover the subject at home. While "sex education" is a secular way to present the biological facts of life, "sexuality education" is the better approach. Because the act of sex involves more than the biology, sexuality education must encompass the whole human person, and can never be divorced from education in love and virtue.

When talking to your children about human sexuality, keep in mind that each child, each gender, and each age has different developmental needs.[159] Don't force a child's sexual maturation, but rather, observe and nurture it with information given in the right way and at the right time. But a parent must also guard against naiveté with regard to their teens. In a disturbing study of 700 teenagers, 58 percent of the teens reported being sexually active, but only one-third of the mothers believed they were.[160]

The years of innocence

In early childhood, your sons and daughters will enjoy years of wonder and innocence, free from any interest in the opposite sex. If only this stage could last through high school! This phase of development typically lasts until the start of puberty.[161] During this time, a child has a God-given right to enjoy innocence. If he is presented with inappropriate sexual information during this time, he will lack the maturity to properly understand and assimilate what is being presented to him. Premature sexual information can be damaging to the emotional and educational development of a child.[162]

The Catholic Church states,

> In general, the first sexual information to be given to a small child does not deal with genital sexuality, but rather with pregnancy and the birth of a brother or sister. The child's natural curiosity is stimulated, for example, when it sees the signs of pregnancy in its mother and experiences waiting for a baby. Parents can take advantage of this happy experience in order to communicate some simple facts about pregnancy, but always in the deepest context of wonder at the creative work of God, who wants the new life he has given to be cared for in the mother's body, near her heart.[163]

During this phase you should use indirect ways to form your child in chastity. For example, teach her about love, respect, the gift of life, the sacredness of her body, and proper physical boundaries. Thankfully, many good books and other resources have been created to help parents teach their children about these essential topics.[164] Even at a young age, you can help form your child's conscience and help him to grow in virtue and self-control. For example, when you help your child in the bath or restroom, you can introduce the ideas of privacy and modesty.

Even complex ideas such as delayed gratification and impulse control can be taught to a pre-schooler. More than 40 years ago, a Stanford psychologist studied 400 four-year-olds to measure how they would respond to a tempting situation. The scientist, Walter Mischel, had each child sit at a desk and placed a single marshmallow in front of him, giving him a choice: eat the treat now, or wait a few minutes and get a second marshmallow. After making sure the child understood, the researcher left the room and watched the child through a one-way mirror. Some immediately gobbled up the snack. Others waited patiently to receive their reward. Some covered their eyes, because they could not bear the sight of the temptation. Others kicked the desk, tugged on their pigtails, and stroked the marshmallow as if it were a stuffed animal

Mischel followed the same children for 14 years to see if the ability to delay gratification had a positive affect on their life-outcomes. What he discovered was that those who could practice impulse control and delayed gratification had the habits of successful people, resulting in more successful marriages, higher incomes, greater career satisfaction, better health and more fulfilling lives. Those who were unable to resist the allure of the marshmallow were more troubled, stubborn, indecisive, and less confident. They also scored, on average, 210 points lower on their SAT. Because they lacked the discipline and focus to resist instant gratification, they had difficulty achieving long-range goals.[165]

While this study does not mean that your child is doomed to an unsuccessful life if he can't abstain from treats, it does afford parents with a simple tool to begin teaching the basic principles of chastity. If you refrain from something good now, you can obtain something great later. This simple principle—delayed gratification—is a secret to success in any area of life, whether it be morality, athletics, financial matters, or even spirituality.

During the age of innocence, you should also talk to your child about why he or she should be proud of being a boy or a girl. When you pray with your child at night, you could say, "Thank you God for making Emily a girl like mommy, and Nicholas a boy like daddy."

Boys should be taught to thank God for their natural ability to protect, provide, lead, and father. The Church states that the pre-pubescent boy "should learn that, although it must be considered as a divine gift, his masculinity is not a sign of superiority with regard to women, but a call from God to take on certain roles and responsibilities."[166] Meanwhile, girls should be taught to thank God for their natural ability to love, nurture, and mother. This gratitude is increasingly important in a world that minimizes the difference between the sexes and sometimes labels gender as meaningless or something that can be chosen.

In the same respect, don't give in to negative stereotypes such as the idea that boys should never show emotion or that girls are incapable of intellectual accomplishments or going to work, or that motherhood is less valuable than a "career." Children need to be taught to be grateful for who they are.

As an important side note, if your child shows signs of gender identity disorder in the years of innocence or same-sex attraction as he enters adolescence, this is something that at times, and with appropriate intervention, *can* be corrected early on, despite the claims of homosexual lobbying groups. Seek out a faithful Catholic or Christian counselor and check out narth. com or catholiccounselors.com for information. And while ever guiding, never stop loving and accepting your child right where he is.[167]

Parents must be aware that the topic of homosexuality is becoming more prevalent in the lives of today's young people. One popular pop-song by a female artist has the lyrics, "I kissed a girl, and I liked it . . . I kissed a girl just to try it. I hope my boyfriend don't mind it. It felt so wrong. It felt so right. Don't mean I'm in love tonight. . . . No, I don't even know your name. It doesn't matter. You're my experimental game. Just human nature. It's not what good girls do. Not how they should behave. My head gets so confused. Hard to obey. . . . Ain't no big deal it's innocent."[168] "I Kissed a Girl" topped the charts in more than 20 countries and had over 25 million views on YouTube. Because the celebration of "diversity," tolerance, and sexual experimentation has become commonplace, today's parents have a unique task in ensuring that their children have healthy ideas about human sexuality.

Puberty

When your child hits puberty (or rather, when puberty hits your child like a two-by-four) the years of innocence come to a screeching halt and the awkwardness of adolescence begins. Your home is awash in a wave of teen hormones. Have your surfboard ready. Puberty is packed with potential, both good and bad, which calls for parents to be more involved than ever in their child's moral and spiritual formation.

During this time, you will need to teach your child directly and delicately about sex—starting with explanations of the changes occurring in his or her body.[169] But continue to prayerfully follow the cues of your developing child regarding when and how. For instance, your daughter might be ready to be taught about feminine hygiene long before the details of sexual intercourse. In fact, she'll probably be ready to learn some details about her menstrual/fertility cycle before being taught about sex. When the time comes to present the birds and the bees, make sure to emphasize the beauty and dignity of the source of human life. In other words, always present sexuality within the context of life and love.

Young women should be made aware of how their fertility cycle functions, and how this will affect them physically and emotionally. They should see this time in life as a doorway to womanhood, unafraid and unashamed of the biological symphony that God has orchestrated within them. They should also feel a sense of pride in the privilege that belongs solely to women to bear life. Use this lesson to remind them about how sacred and beautiful they are in God's eyes and yours, and that the gift of their sexuality needs to be guarded from whatever—or whoever—might degrade it.

It is crucial to reinforce the message of modesty as your girl's body develops. Make it clear that you aren't trying to make her look unattractive and frumpy, but dignified. If the clothes you offer her look like potato sacks with holes cut out for arms, that won't help your case! See the end of this booklet for Web sites that feature beautiful and modest clothing, even for high-school dances.

The way your daughter dresses should reflect the dignity you see in her—the dignity she needs to remember within herself. It needs to send the message that she is worthy of respect. If it doesn't, she most likely won't get it. If she doesn't grasp this (or pretends not to) use your parental authority to place limits on what she can and cannot wear, and don't assume that school uniforms solve the issue. Not much needs to be said about the skirt length (or lack thereof) allowed in many private schools!

Boys during puberty will be struggling with sexual desire.[170] Without guidance, a young man can easily develop patterns of sexual sin that can shape and dominate his whole life. One example is that most boys (and even many girls) fall into the habit of masturbation as their bodies begin to develop. Some parents dismiss this as harmless and inevitable. However, while a teenager's immaturity can lessen the personal guilt of such a sin, the act cannot be morally justified.[171] Masturbation is disordered and could lead to a pattern of grave sin, self-centeredness, and borderline addictive behavior into adulthood. The Church states that "adolescents should be helped to overcome manifestations of this disorder, which often express the inner conflicts of their age and, in many cases, a selfish vision of sexuality."[172]

Elsewhere, the Church notes that

One cannot give what one does not possess. If the person is not master of self—through the virtues and, in a concrete way, through chastity—he or she lacks that self-possession which makes self-giving possible. *Chastity is the spiritual power which frees love from selfishness and aggression.* To the degree that a person weakens chastity, his or her love becomes more and more selfish, that is, satisfying a desire for pleasure and no longer self-giving.[173]

Teens who engage in masturbation are often ashamed, but they sometimes feel incapable of breaking free from it. By talking to your teen about this subject, or at least giving him reading material that addresses the issue as it relates to chastity,[174] you are helping your sons and daughters to be free to love. Fathers, especially, need to be close to their sons during puberty, reminding them of God's high purpose for his desires—marital love and new life. Without being overbearing or violating his sense of privacy, guide him on the path to authentic manhood. He needs you.

Having the talk

When it comes time to present the facts of life, mothers should take the predominant role in speaking to the daughters, while the father takes on the main role in speaking to the sons. This does not mean that the mother remains silent with her sons or that the dad never talks with his girls about human sexuality and chastity in general. Because sexuality is a male/female issue, teens need to hear from both parents. But when talking more specifically about the sexual act, mom-to-daughter and father-to-son is the most sensitive route.

If you are a single parent with a child of the opposite sex, you may want to consider finding someone you trust of the same sex as your child.[175] A relative, pastor, or youth minister may be a helpful advocate in your efforts to present the message of sexuality. However, don't be discouraged from believing that you can effectively promote chastity to your teen.

When teaching about sex, keep it simple. With clear, unambiguous language, tell your child what sex is and how it brings about new life. Never give more information than is needed. Never teach using pictures that are in any way erotic, and keep in mind that it doesn't take much for a teenage boy to find something erotic.[176] You also don't need to explain every sexual disorder plaguing humanity.

To understand sexual ethics, your child needs to first understand God's plan for human sexuality. Without knowing the purpose of sex (babies and bonding) your child will never be able to adequately understand the immorality of sexual sins, including fornication, homosexual acts, masturbation, and contraception.

When teaching about sex, keep it sacred. As the Church says, "Human sexuality is a sacred mystery."[177] That truth isn't only communicated by words, but by the way you teach. Never trivialize this topic. Don't let your awkwardness drive you to make inappropriate jokes. Always use modesty, reverence, and respect when talking about sex with your child, and keep drawing the conversation back to God's purpose for sex.

God created sex to bring new life into the world and to unite a married couple in love. He created human sexuality as a way to stamp the fundamental vocation of every human being into our very bodies—our vocation to give ourselves to others in love. The male body simply doesn't make sense if there is not "an other" to give himself to. The reverse is also true. Because we are made in the image and likeness of the God who is love, we are incomplete when we fail to live in love. "[M]an . . . cannot fully find himself except through a sincere gift of himself."[178]

This vocation to love is lived out in our everyday lives, and also through the specific vocations of marriage or celibacy (i.e. priesthood and religious life). Married couples live out their sexuality through the marital act, in which they physically express the gift of their lives to each other in life-giving love. By doing so, they become an earthly reflection of the life-giving love of God. Meanwhile, priests and religious sisters express their call to make a gift of themselves in life-giving love through the gift of their lives in service and sacrifice for the Church. A teen lives out the truth of his sexuality through abstinence. By remaining pure, a boyfriend expresses love for his girlfriend by doing what is best for her. The girlfriend does the same through her exercise of virtue. They make a gift of themselves through their sacrifice of purity and self-control. This is not the repression of love but a true expression of it.

Find the balance between speaking and listening.

If you don't overcome your insecurities and talk to your teen about matters regarding sexuality, he'll never feel comfortable talking to you about his struggles. As a result, you'll miss out on chances to help him avoid dangerous situations. Look for teachable moments and use them. Such moments are all too abundant. They don't only present themselves in the drama of daily life at high school or the development occurring in his body, but in the culture at large.

Because today's culture saturates everyone with an inglorious portrayal of sexuality on billboards, commercials, and bumper stickers, it's impossible to avoid the subject. The problem has become so universal that a parent can easily feel overwhelmed and discouraged. However, instead of giving in to despair or frustration, use the false portrayals of human sexuality as an opportunity to teach the truth. For example, when you notice your teen glancing at a tabloid magazine in the grocery store check-out line, feel free to chime in about how the sexual scandal in the headlines illustrates how deeply confused Hollywood is when it comes to making love last in real life.

While it's essential to get over your insecurities when it comes to speaking to your teens about sexuality, it's also important to know when to take a break. Not everything needs to be turned into a lecture about life lessons, and sometimes a parent needs to pass on the chance to squeeze in a morality speech. Instead of talking, consider asking them what they think of a particular issue. Listen to them, and try to ask the right questions. Who knows, they might even speak to you, especially if they see that you enjoy their company.

The communication gap can be frustrating at times, but be patient. Numerous studies show that teens want better relationships with their parents, but nobody needs to see a peer-reviewed scientific journal to notice that they hardly act like it. Nonetheless, nearly 70 percent of teens said it would be easier for them to abstain from sex if they could have more open and honest conversations about the topic with their parents.[179] Not surprisingly, teens who talk to their parents about sex typically wait longer to begin having sex, and have fewer partners.[180] Therefore, follow the advice of the Church when it recommends that you teach them yourself, "before they get this information from their companions or from persons who are not well-intentioned."[181]

Burnout prevention

When presenting the profound and inseparable truths of the theology and biology of the body, be mindful that your child is affected by concupiscence (our tendency toward sin and lack of self-control, due to original sin). Also keep in mind that she is growing up in a society where people's bodies are ready for sex long before they are emotionally and financially ready for marriage. Chastity is no easy path! Expect greatness, but be open and honest about this fact.

Your children need to know that God loves them and is patient with them as they fight the good fight. If they don't internalize this, they may burn out, despair, and buckle under the weight of temptation. If you sense your child is struggling, make sure he knows it is understandable to fall down and get up again as he climbs the path toward authentic love. Go to confession with your child regularly. Doing so will save him from feelings of isolation and shame and provide him with powerful graces. Confession is not merely a good habit in the spiritual life, but is urgent and essential if your child has committed a grave sin.

Teens also need to know that while chastity is a battle, it is not a battle *against* sexual desire, as if it were somehow inherently evil. Sexual desire is a gift from God. The struggle for chastity is not simply to defeat, but to protect, purify, and reserve the biological impulse for sex for the noble purpose God gives it.

If you're suspicious that your teen is sexually active, you can't afford to be quiet. Ask questions, but in a way that makes her feel safe giving you an honest answer. If it's confirmed (by her, or by the birth control you found . . . no, she wasn't keeping that for her friend), take her to church for a good confession and to the doctor for a good checkup. Just as some sins can be mortal and require immediate spiritual healing, some STDs can destroy a person's fertility if not treated in time. Don't delay, but take the necessary measures to bring healing to your teen's body and soul.

You *are* qualified

Many parents feel overwhelmed and under-qualified when it comes to teaching their teens about love, relationships, and sexuality. It's okay to feel like you're in over your head, because you are! In fact, you've been in over your head from the moment your first child was born. But you are *not* under-qualified, regardless of your situation. Single parents do have some disadvantages, but they also have the advantage of teaching through example. After all, you're not asking anything of your teen that you're not practicing yourself.

Remember that you don't have to be an expert to talk about any of this with your child. In fact, a little awkwardness can be a good thing. That will help convey to your child that this isn't a mathematical topic that can be presented with textbook precision, but is something that requires a personal and genuine delivery.

You are not disqualified to talk to your teen about sex and chastity if you failed at it yourself in the past. Your authority does not come from your perfection but from your parenthood, which comes from God. Your failures actually can serve to your advantage. Think of it this way: If you had declared bankruptcy as a young couple, would you think you have no place to tell your child to stop maxing out his new credit card? Certainly not! No, you'd be able to sympathize with his temptation and you'd be even more anxious to help him *not* repeat your mistakes.

You might not have the perfect past (which, by the way, is none of your child's business). You might not be the most gifted communicator. But you bear the great and awesome titles, "Dad" or "Mom." You know and can influence your child more effectively than anyone else on earth. Give them the truth and meaning of human sexuality. They are dying to hear it—and they might literally die if they don't.

Your teens want to know what love is, how to find it, how to receive it, and how to give it. Therefore, they need straight answers to their tough questions. One of the most common reasons teens become sexually active is the lack of a convincing reason to wait. One college student admitted that she entirely failed at chastity because she could never answer the question, "Why wait?"

Your teens, however, probably won't ask you all their deepest questions. Therefore, give them solid resources to fill their curious minds with the truth. At our Web site, chastityproject.com, we offer numerous books, CDs, DVDs, and a curriculum that will help you bring the message of chastity to your teens. You are not alone in this task. Ask at your parish or Catholic school for resources and people who can help you. Also, check out the links we provide in the resource section at the end of this book.

If you don't talk to your children about sexuality, love, and relationships, the world will fill the void of your silence with a very contrary message. All the powers of hell are anxious to deform the image of the God of love in your child. If not from you, your child will learn about sex from MTV, friends, Web sites, movies, and magazines. As one anti-drug campaign said, "If you're not telling them no, you're telling them yes."

Your love for your children and your unique relationship with them makes you more qualified to teach them about the truth and meaning of human sexuality than anyone else. As we stated at the start of this book, *no one* has the power to influence your teen's choices as much as you—and with power comes the responsibility to use it. So, make sure that you don't simply muster up the courage to have "the talk" with your child—have hundreds.

GROUP STUDY QUESTIONS:

1. Did your parents talk to you about sex? What was that experience like? If they didn't, from whom did you learn about the birds and the bees?

2. In raising your children, when did you know it was time for "the talk"?

3. When giving your child the facts of life, were there things you wish you would have said or done differently? What seemed to work well?

4. Do you feel comfortable talking to your teen about chastity? What scares you most about addressing this topic with your child? Do you think your teen feels safe coming to you about this subject?

5. How can you foster more open, yet reverent, lines of communication with your child on this subject?

10.

Model chastity in marriage.

"Be imitators of me, as I am of Christ."
(1 Cor 11:1)

"Actions speak louder than words; let your words
teach and your actions speak. . . . It is useless for
a man to flaunt his knowledge of the law if he
undermines its teaching by his actions."
—St. Anthony of Padua

It is not enough to encourage teens to abstain from sexual activity until marriage: That merely promotes abstinence (the absence of sex). As Christian parents, our goal is to instill in them the virtue of chastity.

Like all virtues, chastity is easier caught than taught. If we want our boys to learn to respect women, they don't need books about chivalry. They need to watch how their dad treats their mom. If we want them to be humble, they need to see us ask *their* forgiveness when we fail to love them. In the same respect, if we want them to practice chastity, the best thing we can do for them is to model the virtue within marriage.

To many, the concept of "chastity within marriage" is a strange idea. Often, the term chastity is confused with abstinence or celibacy. While abstinence is the absence of sex and celibacy is a religious vow to remain abstinent, chastity is the strength to use God's gift of sexuality according to his designs. All people are called to live chastely, regardless of their state in life (married, single, or religious). For the married couple, chastity means following God's plan in the bedroom (some think this room is exempt), and treating one another as gifts, not objects to use or take for granted. For the single person, chastity means reserving for marriage the forms of affection appropriate for husbands and wives. For a priest and other consecrated celibates, it involves the fulfillment of their vows of celibacy. For everyone, it involves purity of mind, heart, body, and speech.

Renewing your vows

If chastity is strength to use sexuality according to God's designs, what exactly does this mean for married couples? What are God's designs for sex? One way to understand the act of lovemaking is to see it as the wedding vows made flesh. When a husband and wife stand at the altar on their wedding day, they make several promises to one another. They promise that their union is *free*, *total*, *faithful*, and *open to life*. On the night of their wedding, they will renew these vows, but through the language of their bodies:

- The sexual union of husband and wife ought to be *free*. It cannot be coerced or manipulated. While some spouses struggle with vices that lead them to be dominated by selfish desire, others struggle with wounds that lead them to withhold themselves. Both extremes should be overcome with patience and prayer, because the sexual act ought to be freely given and freely received. Otherwise, it contradicts the very essence of married love.

- The sexual union of husband and wife ought to be *total*. Because it requires a complete gift of self, it cannot be conditional. Nor should anything be held back, including fertility.

- The sexual union ought to be *faithful*. This means more than just avoiding adultery. It means avoiding the unfaithfulness of the eyes, of speech, and of imagination. This demands that the marriage be free of pornography, swimsuit magazines, immodest romance novels, flirting with others, lust, emotional affairs, and anything else that violates the vow to be true to one another.
- The sexual union ought to be *open to life*. The promise of newlyweds to welcome children into their marriage should not be contradicted when they renew their wedding vows through the marital embrace. God designed sex to have two purposes: life and love (babies and bonding). To sterilize an act of love while seeking only bonding is like engaging in intercourse only for the sake of procreation, while attempting to avoid all emotional attachment. Neither action conforms to God's designs for the gift of sexuality. That is why the Church forbids couples from deliberately sterilizing their acts of intercourse, whether temporarily by means of contraception or permanently through surgical sterilization.

When a husband and wife love each other with a free, total, faithful, and life-giving love, they become an earthly image of the creative and unconditional love of God. For this reason, St. Paul said that the one-flesh union of a married couple is a great mystery with reference to Christ and the Church (Eph 5:31-32). God's plan for us to love as he loves is stamped into our very being, and so there is really only one question to ask when it comes to sexual morality: "Am I expressing God's love through my body?"

Upon reading all this theology, some may think, "I'm all in favor of being faithful to my spouse and loving him or her unconditionally, but don't you think the Church is overstepping its bounds by expecting us to throw away our birth control and have an enormous family?"

The Church cannot choose your family size for you. All the Church asks is that if you wish to regulate the number of children you have, make the decision prayerfully and with generosity and then use means that are not contraceptive. The Church is not opposed to couples regulating the number of children they have; what the Church is opposed to is *contraception*, when a couple engages in the marital act but deliberately blocks or even destroys its life-giving potential.

How is a couple to regulate family size without contraception? Thankfully, God has built into every woman's cycle a monthly season of fertility and infertility. By using Natural Family Planning (NFP), a couple can avoid or achieve pregnancy by observing the changes in a woman's body that indicate her fertility. Any couple can pinpoint the woman's time of ovulation and space births by abstaining from sex during the fertile period. Not to be confused with the outdated and ineffective calendar/rhythm method, modern NFP is 99 percent effective when used properly.[182] (See the resource section for information about NFP.) When postponing pregnancy is necessary, NFP is more reliable than condoms and does not require the health risks of hormonal contraception or the regrettable permanence of sterilization.

Natural Family Planning is *not* a "Catholic form of contraception" because God's natural design for each act of sex is respected and not contradicted. Refraining from intercourse is not the same as sterilizing an act of intercourse.

Many people dismiss the idea of using NFP because they assume it's unreliable and ineffective. Others don't care to explore the possibility of using it because it requires times of abstinence. Countless married couples enter marriage with a mistaken notion that chastity and abstinence are things that apply only to singles. But in every marriage, abstinence has its place, whether due to an exhausted spouse, travel, sickness, or any number of other reasons. Healthy marriages survive these times and grow stronger, and NFP couples know from experience that the times apart can serve to draw them closer together. (As a side-note to any concerned spouses, research shows that NFP couples do not have intercourse less often than other couples. They just time it differently.[183])

Couples who use NFP often report that the practice of self-control keeps them from taking each other for granted. Since the spouses are not constantly sexually "available" to the other, the relationship is given space to breathe. In the words of one husband, "[I]t's wonderful because it almost creates the honeymoon over and over again."[184] Another husband explained, "[NFP] has called me to cherish my wife rather than simply desire her."[185] The Church echoes these remarks, saying that NFP, "favors attention for one's partner, helps both parties to drive out selfishness, the enemy of true love, and deepens their sense of responsibility."[186] NFP helps couples (specifically, men) to work on other ways of communicating affection. The short period of abstinence required every month can also bring up relationship issues that may need attention. Sometimes sexual intimacy covers up such problem areas that require a more substantial resolution.

The Church is not opposed to contraception because it is artificial. After all, it allows the use of countless artificial drugs and other technological advances that heal dysfunction and promote the proper functioning of the body. Contraception does the opposite: It prevents the proper and healthy functioning of one bodily system (the reproductive system), inducing or simulating a dysfunctional state (sterility). On the other hand, couples who practice NFP respect God's purpose for sex, including a woman's fertility, and work *with* that plan to space births.

One husband remarked that there are legitimate reasons to delay pregnancy:

> But God has taken care of that already. So deeply has he wrought his purposes into us that a woman's body not only bears fruit, but has seasons . . . providing not only for bringing babies forth, but for spacing them. There is no need to thwart the design, to artificially block fertility during a naturally fertile time. One only has to wait for a few days. If that is too difficult for us, something is wrong.[187]

Practice what you preach

Living chastity within marriage is not easy. Sometimes it can be a very demanding sacrifice. But *you cannot expect your teen to practice chastity outside of marriage if you are unwilling to practice it within marriage.* Consider what the virtue of chastity demands for a teen: They must stand in opposition to the media, resist mockery from peers, risk rejection from potential dates, and possibly place their entire social status on the line. Parents don't have as much at stake. At times, it does involve an element of risk because one's spouse may not be open to the idea. However, neighbors aren't going to mock you for using NFP. Nobody is going to make fun of you at homeowner association meetings because you practice chastity in marriage.

For married couples, the pressure is not external. It is a matter of the heart and the will. A couple must ask themselves, "Is God truly the center of our marriage? Are we willing to give him lordship over every part of our relationship?" This requires faith, humility, and a spirit of generosity and love of God. But God is never outdone in goodness and he will certainly bless those who obey him.

The parents, in turn, become a blessing for their children. When a husband and wife practice chastity in marriage it shows in countless ways. They become living witnesses of the qualities they hope to instill in their teens. To be chaste requires patience, obedience to the will of God, and recourse to the Holy Spirit for strength. But are these not the same things that chastity demands from a high-school student? Consider the reasoning of a teen who becomes sexually active: "I don't need to obey the Church. It's not a big deal. We really love each other. I can make my own decisions with my sexuality. After all, it's my body." It is not a coincidence that these same arguments are made by married couples who disregard the Church's teaching on contraception.

The secret of living a pure life must first be understood by the parents. They must know—from experience—what it means to deny themselves for the good of another and to refrain from immediate pleasures in order to do the will of God. In the words of Mother Teresa, NFP "is nothing more than self-control out of love for each other."[188]

However, chastity in marriage does not simply mean that couples use Natural Family Planning instead of contraception. What is needed is a return to a truly Catholic understanding of marriage, family, and sexuality. The Church teaches,

> Married life also entails a joyous and demanding path to holiness. . . . Parents are well aware that *living conjugal chastity themselves* is the most valid premise for educating their children in chaste love and in holiness of life. . . . At the center of the spirituality of marriage . . . lies chastity, not only as a moral virtue (formed by love), but likewise as a virtue connected with the gifts of the Holy Spirit—*above all the gift of respect for what comes from God.*[189]

This is an extraordinary statement—that chastity lies at the very center of the spirituality of marriage. The core of this issue is the couple's posture toward God: Do we receive our married life as a sacred gift from God or as something we "own," are entitled to, and can manipulate as we wish? When couples realize this and live it out in their lives, they become the most potent antidote against the forces that undermine their children's innocence. Practicing chastity in marriage is not a guarantee that your children will be saints. However, parents must never forget that although our children will not always obey us, they will never fail to imitate us.

The chaste and unconditional love between a husband and wife is the most convincing witness against the culture's empty promises offered by promiscuity. To persevere in purity, teens need to see this big picture. They need to understand that their consistent "no's" to a life of sin are actually a resounding "yes" to authentic love. If God is calling them to the sacrament of marriage, then they're not simply waiting for a sacrament; they're waiting for their future spouse. The witness of your marital love can convey this more powerfully than anything else.

One girl shared with us why she wanted to save herself for marriage. She recalled, "One day, my dad walked up behind my mother and gave her a huge hug. Looking over her shoulder into my eyes, he said, "Maggie, all I hope for you is that one day you find a man who loves you as much as I love your mother." After hearing that, how could she settle for any less? No one needed to tell her about love. She saw it with her own eyes.

The family must be the guide. Pope John Paul II said of his father, "*His example was in a way my first seminary*, a kind of domestic seminary."[190] Likewise, it could be said that your child's first marriage-preparation class is witnessing your marriage. The Church teaches,

> Formation for true love is always the best preparation for the vocation to marriage. In the family, children and young people can learn to live human sexuality within the solid context of Christian life. They can gradually discover that a stable Christian marriage cannot be regarded as a matter of convenience or mere sexual attraction. By the fact that it is a vocation, marriage must involve a carefully considered choice, a mutual commitment before God and the constant seeking of his help in prayer.[191]

GROUP STUDY QUESTIONS:

1. During your marriage preparation, was the Church's teaching on chastity within marriage ever explained to you?

2. In what ways is chastity *in* marriage just as challenging as chastity *prior* to marriage?

3. How has NFP been a blessing in your marriage? If you don't practice it, how do you think it could be a blessing?

4. How can practicing chastity within marriage (or as a single adult) help you raise chaste teens?

5. In what ways has your marriage taught your child the meaning of love?

CONCLUSION

Children don't learn who they are by looking in a mirror. Perhaps newborns can only see from our arms to our faces because God wants them to learn who they are by looking into the faces of their mother and father. They learn that their identity and worth doesn't depend on their accomplishments, nor is it negated by their failures. They learn that they are precious—that they are worth dying for, just because they are yours.

We as parents are not only the primary educators, but also the primary *evangelists* of our children. Their experience of our love is what gives them the capacity to grasp the love of God the Father for them.[192] You are the image of divine love for your children. You are his protective hand keeping them from harm. You are his mercy, catching them when they fall and finding them when they want to be left alone in sin. Therefore, the family is rightly called "the school of love."

Children learn from their heavenly Father's love, mirrored in our faces, that they are not defined by their faults, failures, school gossip, or confusion. They are defined by the love of God for them, which teaches them that they are worth far more than a few dates, a fancy dinner, or making it to the prom. God proclaimed their enormous price tag on the cross and in the Eucharist. In God's estimation, they are worth his life.

The sense of dignity our children receive from God and us will form the foundation of the respect and boundaries they demand from others. That sense of dignity and love will also give them the courage to get up if they fall, because they'll know that they are worth more than what they just did.

We all hope our children don't have to learn the lessons of this book the hard way. But in the end, they have free will. Without free will, the radical possibility of love wouldn't exist. But love's opposite, by necessity, is always a possibility as well.

No matter where they go, be patient with them and with yourself, and continue to love them unconditionally. Love without conditions is a love that might inspire guilt, but will never inspire a shame that leads to despair. It's a love that will empower our children to feel safe coming to us for help no matter what they've done. It's a love that is patient with weakness while never ceasing to demand greatness. It's the love that God shows us. But you have to be convinced of that love yourself. Therefore, don't forget the love your heavenly Father has for *you*. And don't forget that you're not alone in the battle to raise pure teens. After all, your children are God's children too.

GROUP STUDY QUESTIONS:

1. What are two concrete ways in which you can begin to promote chastity within your family?
2. Regarding the topic of sexuality and chastity, what do you wish someone had conveyed to you when you were a teenager?
3. Did you grow up knowing unconditional love from your parents? From God?
4. If unconditional love was lacking in your childhood, what can you do to strengthen your own sense of self-worth now?
5. How can you more effectively show unconditional love to your child?

Resources

For parents

- *Parenting for Purity* (CD)
  By Jason Evert
  Parents are the primary sex educators
  for their children, but many are uncomfortable
  with this responsibility because they don't know
  where to begin. Jason provides excellent tips and
  advice for preventing teens from falling into
  damaging lifestyles. Parents will come to realize
  the importance of teaching their children about
  chastity, no matter what their age. (Available at
  chastityproject.com)

- *Pure Intimacy* (Book)
  By Jason Evert
  In this booklet, Jason explains the
  biological, spiritual, and emotional
  benefits of NFP. *Pure Intimacy* will
  help readers understand God's plan for
  the gift of their sexuality and the many
  graces of natural family planing, helping them
  build stronger marriages and thus, stronger
  families. (Available at chastityproject.com)

- *Green Sex* (CD)
  By Jason Evert
  In this CD, Jason explains the role of
  chastity within marriage and why this
  virtue strengthens the love between a man and a
  woman. This talk will help every couple—whether
  newly engaged or already married. (Available at
  chastityproject.com)

- *Relativism: Do You Know How
  it is Affecting You?* (CD)
  By Chris Stefanick
  Pope Benedict XVI has called relativism,
  "the greatest problem of our time," and it's
  a problem you can't afford to ignore! In this
  presentation, Chris will help you understand
  relativism and equip you to meet it head-on.
  (Available at reallifecatholic.com)

- *Youth Cult-ure* (CD)
  By Chris Stefanick
  The postmodern world that young
  people find themselves in provides no
  moral or religious framework to help them make
  sense out of life. It's no wonder that, according to
  a recent Centers for Disease Control survey, 17
  percent of teens have considered suicide. In this

presentation, Chris spells out the cultural factors that have robbed teens of faith and hope, and how you as a parent can give it back to them. (Available at reallifecatholic.com)

- *The New Sexual Revolution: How to Form Pure Teens* (CD)
  By Chris Stefanick
  Few things impact the course of a child's life as much as her choice for purity or promiscuity. In this talk, Chris covers exactly what parents are up against and gives them practical techniques they need to raise pure teens. (Available at reallifecatholic.com)

For teens

- *How to Date Your Soulmate* (CD)
  By Jason Evert
  Your teen likes someone. Now what?
  Most young people have only been told what they're not supposed to do while dating. This CD offers teens ten strategies for how to practice courtship without compromise. (Available at chastityproject.com)

- *How to Find Your Soulmate without Losing Your Soul* (Book)
  By Jason and Crystalina Evert
  This bestselling book is written for women from the ages of 15 and 35, and offers 21 tips on how to navigate through the single years of life. (Available at howtofindyoursoulmate.com)

- *How to Save Your Marriage— Before Meeting Your Spouse* (CD)
  By Jason Evert
  Can you divorce-proof a marriage before it begins? Marriage preparation doesn't start with the engagement. To build the foundation for lasting love, learn what to do before saying "I do." (Available at chastityproject.com)

- *If You Really Loved Me: 100 Questions on Dating, Relationships, and Sexual Purity* (Book)
  By Jason Evert
  This book is a collection of Jason's answers to the top 100 questions he receives from teens around the world. Questions include: How far is too far? How do I tell a guy "no" without hurting his feelings? How do you know when it's love? How do I forgive myself? What's so

bad about porn? Why should I dress modestly? And
94 others. (Available at chastityproject.com)

- *Pure Faith: Book of Prayer*
  (Book)
  By Jason Evert
  Pure Faith is a hardcover devotional,
  written and designed just for teens. It
  contains prayers from the saints,
  prayers for every occasion, and prayers
  to help young people get the most out of Mass,
  confession, and adoration. This book is ideal as a
  gift for confirmation or graduation. (Available at
  chastityproject.com)

- *Pure Love* (Book)
  By Jason Evert
  In an easy-to-read Q & A format, this
  booklet is a great introduction to the
  topic of chastity. Due to its popularity
  in youth groups, confirmation classes,
  and high schools, *Pure Love* has been
  given to hundreds of thousands of teens at
  several World Youth Days. (Available at
  chastityproject.com) (Catholic, Spanish, and
  public school versions are available.)

- *Pure Manhood* (Book)
  By Jason Evert
  Teenage boys are often told to be
  gentlemen and to treat women like
  ladies. However, they are rarely given
  concrete steps on how to do this. In *Pure
  Manhood,* Jason Evert challenges young men
  to look to Christ as the model of masculinity
  and purity. (Available at chastityproject.com)
  (Catholic, Spanish, and public school versions are
  available.)

- *Porn Detox* (CD)
  By Jason Evert
  This CD provides strategies to help men
  conquer their daily temptations with
  lust, with special emphasis on breaking free
  from pornography. If you, or someone you love,
  struggles with pornography or simply lust in
  general, this CD will be a blessing in your battle
  with temptation. (Available at chastityproject.com)

- *Pure Womanhood* (Book)
  By Crystalina Evert
  Every woman longs for love, but many
  have given up. In *Pure Womanhood,*
  Crystalina Evert restores a woman's hope.

By her powerful testimony and blunt words of wisdom, she shows that real love is possible . . . regardless of the past. (Available at chastityproject.com) (Catholic, Spanish, and public school versions are available.)

- *Love or Lust?* (DVD & CD)
  By Jason & Crystalina Evert
  In this high school assembly, Jason Evert and Crystalina Evert use their humor, honesty, and powerful testimonies to provide compelling reasons to pursue a life of purity, regardless of one's past. (Available at chastityproject.com) (Catholic and public school versions are available.)

- *No Imitations! An Invitation to Real Love* (CD)
  By Chris Stefanick
  In this popular chastity assembly, Chris goes beyond fear tactics and "just-say-no's." Instead, he offers teens something to say "Yes!" to—a vision of authentic love, which can only be attained through chastity . . . everything else is an imitation! (Available at reallifecatholic.com)

- *Theology of the Body for Teens*
  (Curriculum with DVD)
  By Jason and Crystalina Evert
  and Brian Butler
  Theology of the Body for Teens
  brings Pope John Paul II's teachings on
  human sexuality into a practical format
  of 12 lessons that teenagers will enjoy and
  understand. This program takes the two hottest
  topics on the planet—God and sex—and "marries"
  them through Pope John Paul II's compelling
  vision for love and life. The curriculum includes a
  student workbook, a leader's guide, a parent guide,
  and a DVD to facilitate the lessons. (Available at
  chastityproject.com)

LINKS:
Chastity Education
- *Abstinence.net* is the Web site of the National
  Abstinence Clearinghouse, an organization that
  offers a wealth of information about promoting
  chastity within schools and communities. Contact
  them if you're looking for an effective abstinence
  curriculum for public schools.
- *Chastityproject.com* is our online resource for
  promoting chastity to teens. On the site, one can
  book seminars, read questions, browse an online

library of audio and video files, and order chastity
resources for teens, parents, and educators.

- *Medinstitute.org* is the Medical Institute of Sexual
  Health, which provides secular medical resources
  to support the message of abstinence. This is a
  helpful tool when convincing public schools of the
  necessity of abstinence education.

Internet and Media Safety

- *Brickhousesecurity.com* offers a number of
  products, including one known as "cell phone
  spy elite" that allows you to retrieve deleted text
  messages from certain cell phones.
- *Bsecure.com* is an Internet filter that can send you
  e-mails letting you know which Web sites people
  in your house have attempted to visit.
- *Covenanteyes.com* is an excellent accountability
  program to help you monitor the activity on
  your computer. (Enter "chastity" as a promo code
  for a discount.)
- *Decentfilms.com* offers movie reviews and
  wholesome recommendations.
- *Internetsafety.com* offers a program called "safe
  eyes" that monitors your child's instant messaging.
  It also can monitor his or her social networking
  sites, and set limits on online minutes.
- *Parentstv.org* educates parents about television

content, aims to improves the quality of prime-time television, and promotes family values. It uses a rating system to measure the moral quality (or lack thereof) of broadcast television programs.

- *Pluggedin.com* is an online resource from Focus on the Family. Here, one can browse reviews of thousands of movies, television shows, video games, and musicians.
- *Websafety.com* offers software to download to your teenagers' phone or computer to see if they're sending inappropriate texts or photos.
- *Chastityproject.com, theporneffect.com,* and *pureintimacy.com* provide helpful tools to help people who struggle with breaking their attachment to pornography.
- *Yoursphere.com* is a social networking Web site that takes stringent measures to prevent predators from intruding into the network. The Web site also monitors and restricts bullying.

Family Life

- *Catholicmoms.com* offers a variety of encouraging resources for mothers, ranging from products and forums to recipes and devotionals.
- *Catholictherapists.com* offers a nationwide resource list of solid Catholic marriage and family counselors.
- *Dads.org* is the Web site of St. Joseph's Covenant

Keepers, a Catholic apostolate that serves and inspires Catholic dads.

- *Family.org* is the Web site of Focus on the Family, an evangelical Christian apostolate that offers a wealth of information on raising a Christian family in the modern world.
- *Catholiccounselors.com* is the Web site of The Pastoral Solutions Institute, which provides information to strengthen marriages and families. It also offers tele-counseling services that allow you to receive over-the-phone assistance from Catholic therapists.
- *Thealexanderhouse.org* is an organization that provides resources and services to lower the divorce rate by helping married couples to live God's plan for marriage. Couple-to-couple coaching is also offered online or via phone.

Modesty
- *Beautifullymodest.com* offers modest formal attire for women, including prom and wedding dresses.
- *Purefashion.com* is an organization that offers modesty fashion shows, where teenage runway models witness to the beauty of modesty.

Natural Family Planning
- *Ccli.org* (The Couple to Couple League) provides information, teaching, and support for

couples using or wanting to learn about Natural Family Planning.

- *Naprotechnology.com* is the Web site of the Pope Paul VI Institute for Human Reproduction, which specializes in treating fertility-related health issues. They also teach a highly effective model of NFP and train health care professionals in pro-life medicine.
- *Omsoul.com* (One More Soul) is a Catholic apostolate dedicated to promoting God's plan for marriage, family life, and human sexuality. One More Soul also provides a national directory of pro-life doctors, who do not prescribe birth control. Such physicians are especially helpful when women are seeking alternatives to the birth-control pill when it is recommended for medical reasons.

Church documents on human sexuality (Available at vatican.va)

- *Catechism of the Catholic Church*
  The *Catechism of the Catholic Church* offers an official summary of rich Catholic doctrine that is readily accessible to anyone. For information in the Catechism on chastity and sexual morality, see paragraph numbers 2331–2400. For information on marriage and family life, see paragraphs 1601–1666.
- *Familiaris Consortio (On the Role of the Christian*

Family in the Modern World)
Issued in 1981, this apostolic exhortation of Pope John Paul II explores the nature of marriage and its importance as the first school of love. He explores the crucial role of the family as the fundamental building block of society, which bears a key role in the evangelizing mission of the Church to the world. The document also delves into the problems families are facing and offers solutions on how to resolve them.

- *Humanae Vitae (Of Human Life)*
In 1968, Pope Paul VI issued this prophetic and profound encyclical on the regulation of birth. In it, he reiterated the Church's constant teaching against contraception, provided a vision of God's plan for life and love, and even foretold the ills that would befall society if contraception spread throughout the world.

- *Theology of the Body*
This is a collection of 129 lectures given by Pope John Paul II during his Wednesday audiences between 1979 and 1984. These teachings form the first major catechesis of his pontificate, and have already begun to revolutionize the way that the Church's teachings on human sexuality are being proclaimed and understood. Today, the collection of lectures can be found in the book *Man and*

Woman He Created Them: A Theology of the Body.
According to Pope John Paul II's biographer,
George Weigel, these lectures "constitute a kind of
theological time bomb set to go off with dramatic
consequences, sometime in the third millennium
of the Church."

- *The Truth and Meaning of Human Sexuality*
Because of the widespread use of "sex education"
in schools, in 1995 the Pontifical Council for
the Family addressed this document primarily
to parents. This offers helpful guidelines for
sexuality education within the family and reiterates
the Church's position that parents are the
primary sex educators of their children. Specific
recommendations are provided to help parents in
this essential task.

ENDNOTES

1   "35,000 Text Messages In A Month," The Associated Press (15 January 2009).

2   Internet Pornography Statistics, Jerry Ropelato. http://Internet-filter-review.topten-reviews.com/Internet-pornography-statistics

3   Weinstock H, et. al., "Sexually Transmitted Diseases among American Youth: Incidence and Prevalence Estimates, 2000," *Perspectives on Sexual and Reproductive Health* 36:1 (2004): 6-10.

4   P. Zollo, *Getting Wiser to Teens: More Insights Into Marketing to Teenagers.* 3rd ed. (Ithaca, N.Y.: New Strategist Publications, 2003).

5   Bill Albert, "With One Voice (lite): A 2009 Survey of Adults and Teens on Parental Influence, Abstinence, Contraception, and the Increase in the Teen Birth Rate," The National Campaign to Prevent Teen and Unplanned Pregnancy, (Spring 2009).

6   The Pontifical Council for the Family, *The Truth and Meaning of Human Sexuality* (Boston: Pauline Books and Media, 1996), 41-47.

7   R. Eng and W. T. Butler, *The Hidden Epidemic: Confronting Sexually Transmitted Diseases* (Washington, D.C.: National Academy Press, 1997), 71-73; "Pelvic Inflammatory Disease," Fact Sheet (CDC); A.B. Moscicki, et al., "Differences in Biologic Maturation, Sexual Behavior, and Sexually Transmitted Disease Between Adolescents with and without Cervical Intraepithelial Neoplasia," *Journal of Pediatrics* 115:3 (September 1989): 487-493; A.B. Moscicki, et al., "The Significance of Squamous Metaplasia in the Development of Low Grade Squamous Intraepithelial Lesions in Young Women," *Cancer* 85:5 (1 March 1999): 1139-1144; M.L. Shew, et al., "Interval Between Menarche and First Sexual Intercourse, Related to Risk of Human Papillomavirus Infection," *Journal of Pediatrics* 125:4 (October 1994): 661-666; Vincent Lee, et al., "Relationship of Cervical Ectopy to Chlamydia Infection in Young Women," *Journal of Family Planning and Reproductive Health Care* 32:2 (April 2006): 104-106.

8   Eileen F. Dunne, et al., "Prevalence of HPV Infection Among Females in the United States," *The Journal of the American Medical Association* 297:8 (28 February 2007): 815-816.

9   Robert E. Rector, et al., "Sexually Active Teenagers are More Likely to be Depressed and to Attempt Suicide," The Heritage Foundation (3 June 2003).

10   Hallfors, et al., "Adolescent Depression and Suicide Risk: Association with Sex and Drug Behavior," *American Journal of Preventive Medicine* 27:3 (October 2004): 224-231; Martha W. Waller, et al., "Gender Differences in Associations Between Depressive Symptoms and Patterns of Substance Use and Risky Sexual Behavior among a Nationally Representative Sample of U.S. Adolescents," *Archives of Women's Mental Health* 9:3 (May 2006): 139-150.

11   D. P. Orr, M. Beiter, G. Ingersoll, "Premature Sexual Activity as an Indicator of Psychosocial Risk," *Pediatrics* 87:2 (February 1991): 141-147.

12   Hallfors, et al., "Which Comes First in Adolescence—Sex and Drugs or Depression?" *American Journal of Preventive Medicine* 29:3 (October 2005): 169.

13   Robert E. Rector, et al., "Sexually Active Teenagers are More Likely to be Depressed and to Attempt Suicide," The Heritage Foundation (3 June 2003).

14   Edward O. Laumann, et al., *The Social Organization of Sexuality: Sexual Practices in the United States* (Chicago: University of Chicago Press, 1994), 503.

15   R. Finger, et al., "Association of Virginity at Age 18 with Educational, Economic, Social, and Health Outcomes in Middle Adulthood," *Adolescent & Family Health* 3:4 (2004): 169.

16   Robert E. Rector, et al., "The Harmful Effects of Early Sexual Activity and Multiple Sexual Partners Among Women: A Book of Charts," The Heritage Foundation (26 June 2003).

17   Robert Rector and Kirk A. Johnson, "Teenage Sexual Abstinence and Academic Achievement," The Heritage Foundation, Conference Paper (27 October 2005).

18   Robert Rector and Kirk A. Johnson, "Teenage Sexual Abstinence and Academic Achievement," The Heritage Foundation, Conference Paper (27 October 2005).

19   Centers for Disease Control, "Sexual and Reproductive Health of Persons Aged 10-24 Years — United States, 2002-2007," *Morbidity and Mortality Weekly Report* 58:SS-6 (17 July 2009): Table 26.; Centers for Disease Control, "Youth Risk Behavior Surveillance—United States, 2007," *Morbidity and Mortality Weekly Report* 57:SS-4 (6 June 2008): 97.

20   Centers for Disease Control, "Trends in HIV-Related Behaviors Among High School Students—United States 1991-2005," *Morbidity and Mortality Weekly* 55:31 (11 August 2006): 851-854.

21   Bill Albert, "With One Voice 2007: America's Adults and Teens Sound Off About Teen Pregnancy," The National Campaign to Prevent Teen Pregnancy, (February 2007), 26.

22   Douglas Kirby, "Understanding What Works and What Doesn't In Reducing Adolescent Sexual Risk-Taking," *Family Planning Perspectives* 33:6 (November/December, 2001): 277.

23   Bill Albert, "With One Voice 2007: America's Adults and Teens Sound Off About Teen Pregnancy," The National Campaign to Prevent Teen Pregnancy, (February 2007), 27.

24   "The Girlcott Story," www.wgfpa.org.

25   Pope John Paul II, *Crossing the Threshold of Hope* (New York: Alfred A. Knopf, Inc., 1994), 123.

26   Col. 1:16; Eph 1:21; Thomas Aquinas, *Summa Theologiae*, I:108.

27   Fulton J. Sheen, *Life is Worth Living* (San Francisco, Ignatius Press, 1992), 337.

28   Quoted in St. Alphonsus de Liguori, *The Glories of Mary*, First Part.

29   St. John Vianney, quoted in Paul Thigpen, *A Dictionary of Quotes from the Saints* (Ann Arbor, Mich.: Charis Books, 2001), 145.

30   Mark 9:29.

31   *Revised Standard Version Second Catholic Edition* (San Francisco, Ignatius Press: 2006), 168.

32   Joe Hanley and Jack Manhire, eds., *Classic Quotes of Catholic Spirituality* (Chicago: PLS), 9.

33 http://www.genesit.it/utenti/chiaralux/le_sedi.asp and http://www.focolare.org/En/ sif/2000/20000323e_b.html

34 Bianchi DW, Zickwolf GK, Weil GJ, et al., "Male Fetal Progenitor Cells Persist in Maternal Blood for as Long as 27 Years Postpartum," *Proceedings of the National Academy of Sciences* 93 (1996): 705-708; Evans, "Long-Term Fetal Microchimerism in Peripheral Blood Mononuclear Cell Subsets in Healthy Women and Women with Scleroderma," *Blood* 93:6 (15 March 1999): 2033-2037.

35 Michael Verneris, "Fetal Microchimerism—What Our Children Leave Behind," *Blood* 102:10 (15 November 2003): 3465-3466.

36 Srivatsa, et al., "Maternal Cell Microchimerism in Newborn Tissues," *Journal of Pediatri*cs 142 (2003): 31-33.

37 Father Jean C.J. d'Elbé, *I Believe in Love* (Manchester, New Hampshire: Sophia Institute Press, 2001), 195, 203-204.

38 George Weigel, *Witness to Hope* (New York: Cliff Street Books, 2001), 30.

39 Pope John Paul II, *Gift and Mystery*, 20.

40 Karol Wojtyła, *The Way to Christ* (New York: Harper & Row Publishers, Inc., 1984), 54.

41 Pope Benedict XVI, Address to the Participants in the International Congress organized to Commemorate the 40th Anniversary of "Dei Verbum." Sept. 16, 2005.

42 *Persona Humana*, Sacred Congregation for the Doctrine of the Faith, 12.

43 Fr. Stefano Manelli, *Jesus, Our Eucharistic Love* (Brookings, S.D.: Our Lady of Victory Mission, 1973), 59-60.

44 Father Jean C.J. d'Elbé, *I Believe in Love* (Manchester, New Hampshire: Sophia Institute Press, 2001), 181.

45 Louann Brizendine, *The Female Brain* (New York: Morgan Road Books, 2006), 14.

46 Brizendine, 5.

47 *The Truth and Meaning of Human Sexuality*, 96 (emphasis added).

48 St. Robert Bellarmine, *The Art of Dying Well*, as quoted in R. E. Guiley, *The Quotable Saint* (New York, N.Y.: Checkmark Books, 2002), 135.

49 Fr. Augustine Donegan, as quoted in Emily Stimpson, "Donegan's Wake," *Franciscan Way* (Autumn, 2009), 14.

50 Joe McIlhaney and Freda McKissic Bush, *Hooked* (Chicago, Northfield Publishing: 2008), 19.

51 Douglas Kirby, "Understanding What Works and What Doesn't In Reducing Adolescent Sexual Risk-Taking," *Family Planning Perspectives* 33:6 (November/ December, 2001): 276.

52 Centers for Disease Control, "Youth Risk Behavior Surveillance—United States, 2005," *Morbidity and Mortality Weekly Report* 55:SS-5 (9 June 2006): 20.

53 *The Truth and Meaning of Human Sexuality*, 102.

54 Homily of His Eminence Card. Joseph Ratzinger, Dean of the College of Cardinals, Mass, Pro Eligendo Romano Pontifice, April 18, 2005.

55 Cardinal Joseph Ratzinger, "Fede, verità, tolleranza—Il cristianesimo e le religioni del mondo," (2003). Quote taken from zenit.org (26 September, 2003).

56 Address of His Holiness Pope Benedict XVI to the Participants in the Ecclesial Diocesan Convention of Rome, June 6, 2005.

57   Pope Benedict XVI, *Charity in Truth*, 3.

58   *The Truth and Meaning of Human Sexuality*, 6, 92, 96, 106.

59   Aquinas, *Summa Theologiae*, Iia-IIae, 35. 4, ad 2. *St. Thomas Aquinas: Philosophical Texts*, trans. Thomas Gilby (New York: Oxford University Press, 1960), 275.

60   Pope John Paul II, *Evangelium Vitae*, 12, 23.

61   R.W. Blum and P.M. Rinehart, "Reducing the Risk: Connections that Make a Difference in the Lives of Youth," Division of General Pediatrics & Adolescent Health, University of Minnesota (1997), 28, 30.

62   Christian Smith and Melinda Lundquist Denton, *Soul Searching: The Religious and Spiritual Lives of American Teenagers* (New York: Oxford University Press, 2005), 222-223.

63   Smith and Lundquist Denton, *Soul Searching*, 138.

64   Valerie F. Reyna and Frank Farley, "Is the Teen Brain Too Rational?" *Scientific American Reports* (June 2007), 62.

65   Cf. *Catechism of the Catholic Church*, 1766; Thomas Aquinas, *S Th*, I-II, 26, 4, *corp. art.*

66   John 15:13

67   *The Truth and Meaning of Human Sexuality*, 9.

68   *The Truth and Meaning of Human Sexuality*, 68.2, 73.

69   Cathleeen Falsani, "Hugh Hefner: Man of God?" (available at www.somareview.com/hughhefnermanofgod.cfm)

70   Falsani, "Hugh Hefner: Man of God?"

71   http://www.sttherese.com/Parents.html

72   "The Adolescent Brain—Why Teenagers Think and Act Differently" (available at www.edinformatics.com/news/teenage_brains.htm)

73   Frontline Interview with Jay Giedd, "Inside the Teenage Brain," (available at www.pbs.org/wgbh/pages/frontline/shows/teenbrain/)

74   Anne Moir and David Jessel, *Brain Sex* (New York: Delta, 1992), 69.

75   Centers for Disease Control, "Youth Risk Behavior Surveillance—United States, 2005," *Morbidity and Mortality Weekly Report* 55:SS-5 (9 June 2006): Table 10.

76   Fisher B.S., Cullen F.T., Turner M.G., "The Sexual Victimization of College Women," Washington: Department of Justice (U.S.), National Institute of Justice; Publication No. NCJ 182369.

77   Tjaden and Thoennes, "Extent, Nature, and Consequences of Intimate Partner Violence: Findings from the National Violence Against Women Survey," U.S. Department of Justice Office of Justice Programs (July 2000), v.

78   "Clinical Management of Survivors of Rape—A Guide to the Development of Protocols for Use in Refugee and Internally Displaced Person Situations," World Health Organization and United Nations High Commissioner for Refugees (March 27-29, 2001): 28.

79   Basile KC, et al., "Prevalence and Characteristics of Sexual Violence Victimization," *Violence and Victims* 22:4 (2007): 437-448.

80   Wonderlich, et al., "Relationship of Childhood Sexual Abuse and Eating Disturbance in Children," *Journal of the American Academy of Child and Adolescent Psychiatry* 39:10 (October 2000): 1277-1283; World Health Organization Report, 2002; Kendler,

et al., "Childhood Sexual Abuse and Adult Psychiatric and Substance Use Disorders in Women," *Archives of General Psychiatry* 57 (2000): 953-959, Table 2.

81 Kendler, et al., "Childhood Sexual Abuse and Adult Psychiatric and Substance Use Disorders in Women," *Archives of General Psychiatry* 57 (2000): 953-959, Table 2.

82 2007 SIECUS National Report; SIECUS National Guidelines for Comprehensive Sexuality Education Kindergarten–12th Grade, and National Guidelines Task Force, The Sexuality Information and Education Council of the United States (SIECUS), 1992.

83 Robert Rector, "The Effectiveness of Abstinence Education Programs in Reducing Sexual Activity Among Youth" The Heritage Foundation (8 April 2002).

84 *Focus on Kids*, University of Maryland, Department of Pediatrics (1998), 137.

85 Kelley Beaucar Vlahos, "CDC-Funded Sex Ed Programs Draw Fire," Fox News (September 09, 2003).

86 Rebecca Hagelin, "Assaulted by Sex-ed," *The Washington Times* (11 August 2009).

87 http://www.plannedparenthoodnj.org/library/topic/sex_education/abstinence_only

88 Robert Rector, "Facts about Abstinence Education," The Heritage Foundation (30 March 2004).

89 Robert E. Rector, Melissa G. Pardue, and Shannan Martin, "What Do Parents Want Taught in Sex Education Programs?" The Heritage Foundation (28 January 2004).

90 Pope John Paul II, *Familiaris Consortio*, 37.

91 Robert Rector, "Facts about Abstinence Education," The Heritage Foundation (March 30, 2004); John B Jemmont, Loretta S. Jemmont, and Geoffrey T. Fong, "Efficacy of a Theory-Based Abstinence-Only Intervention Over 24 Months," *Archives of Pediatric and Adolescent Medicine* 164:2 (February 2010): 152-159.

92 Janet Elise Rosenbaum, "Patient Teenagers? A Comparison of the Sexual Behavior of Virginity Pledgers and Matched Nonpledgers," *Pediatrics* 123:1 (January 2009): e110-e120.

93 William McGurn, "Like a Virgin: The Press Take on Teenage Sex," *The Wall Street Journal*, (6 January 2009), A13.

94 Mathematica Policy Research, Inc. "Impacts of Four Title V, Section 510 Abstinence Education Programs. Final Report," Princeton, NJ. (April, 2007).

95 "'Abstinence Only' Sex Ed Ineffective," Abcnews.com (17 April 2007).

96 Guttmacher Institute's, "State Policies in Brief—as of January 1, 2010: An Overview of Minors' Consent Law."

97 "Abortion: Can't Tell Your Parents? How to Get Help," www.plannedparenthood.org/teen-talk (September, 2009).

98 Suzanne Hoholik, "Pfizer must pay $2.3 billion: Upper Arlington man helped blow whistle on drugmaker's marketing," *The Columbus Dispatch* (3 September 2009).

99 Douglas Kirby, "Understanding What Works and What Doesn't In Reducing Adolescent Sexual Risk-Taking," *Family Planning Perspectives* 33:6 (November/December, 2001): 277.

100 Robert E. Rector, Melissa G. Pardue, and Shannan Martin, "What Do Parents Want Taught in Sex Education Programs?" The Heritage Foundation (28 January 2004).

101 Robert Rector, "Facts about Abstinence Education," The Heritage Foundation (30 March 2004).

102 J. Jaccard, P. Dittus, "Adolescent Perceptions of Maternal Approval of Birth Control and Sexual Risk Behavior," *American Journal of Public Health* 90:9 (September 2000): 1428; cf. J. Jaccard, et al., "Maternal Correlates of Adolescent Sexual Behavior," *Family Planning Perspectives* 28 (1996): 159-165.

103 Bill Albert, "With One Voice 2007: America's Adults and Teens Sound Off About Teen Pregnancy," The National Campaign to Prevent Teen Pregnancy, (February 2007).

104 S. Ahmed S, et al., "HIV Incidence and Sexually Transmitted Disease Prevalence Associated with Condom Use: A Population Study in Rakai, Uganda," *AIDS* 15:16 (2001): 2177.

105 *The Truth and Meaning of Human Sexuality,* note 71.

106 National Institutes of Health, "Scientific Evidence on Condom Effectiveness for Sexually Transmitted Disease (STD) Prevention" (June 2000).

107 L. Manhart, L. Koutsky, "Do Condoms Prevent Genital HPV Infection, External Genital Warts, or Cervical Neoplasia? A Meta-Analysis," *Sexually Transmitted Diseases* 29:11 (2002): 725-735; S. Vaccarella, et al., "Sexual Behavior, Condom Use, and Human Papillomavirus: Pooled Analysis of the IARC Human Papillomavirus Prevalence Surveys," *Cancer Epidemiology Biomarkers & Prevention* 15:2 (2006): 326-333; R. Winer, et al., "Condom Use and the Risk of Genital Human Paillomavirus Infection in Young Women," *The New England Journal of Medicine* 354:25 (2006): 2645-2654; S. Ahmed S, et al., "HIV Incidence and Sexually Transmitted Disease Prevalence Associated with Condom Use: A Population Study in Rakai, Uganda," *AIDS* 15:16 (2001): 2171-2179; J. Baeten, et al., "Hormonal Contraception and Risk of Sexually Transmitted Disease Acquisition: Results from a Prospective Study," *American Journal of Obstetrics & Gynecology* 185:2 (2001): 380-385; J. Shlay, et al., "Comparison of Sexually Transmitted Disease Prevalence by Reported Level of Condom Use Among Patients Attending an Urban Sexually Transmitted Disease Clinic," *Sexually Transmitted Diseases* 31:3 (2004): 154-160; A. Wald, et al., "Effect of Condoms on Reducing the Transmission of Herpes Simplex Virus Type 2 from Men to Women," *The Journal of the American Medical Association* 285:24 (2001): 3100-3106.

108 Cf. National Institutes of Health, "Scientific Evidence on Condom Effectiveness for Sexually Transmitted Disease (STD) Prevention" (June, 2000): 26; House of Representatives, "Breast and Cervical Cancer Prevention and Treatment Act of 1999," November 22, 1999.

109 Division of STD Prevention, "Prevention of Genital HPV Infection and Sequelae: Report of an External Consultants' Meeting," 7.

110 N. Hearst and S. Chen, "Condom Promotion for AIDS Prevention in the Developing World: Is It Working?" *Studies in Family Planning* 35:1 (March 2004): 39-47. (Emphasis mine)

111 Will Ross, "The battle over Uganda's AIDS campaign," BBC News, 12 April, 2005.

112 T. Allen and S. Heald, "HIV/AIDS Policy in Africa: What has Worked in Uganda and What has Failed in Botswana," *Journal of International Development* 16 (2004): 1141-1154. (emphasis mine)

113 UNAIDS "Report on the Global AIDS Epidemic," Annex 2 (2006): 511, 514.

114 Amin Abboud, "Searching for Papal Scapegoats is Pointless," *British Medical Journal* 331 (30 July 2005): 294.

115 Joshua Mann, et al., "The Role of Disease-Specific Infectivity and Number of Disease Exposures on Long-Term Effectiveness of the Latex Condom," *Sexually Transmitted Diseases* 29:6 (June 2002): 344-349; R.E. Bunnell, et al., "High Prevalence and Incidence of Sexually Transmitted Diseases in Urban Adolescent Females Despite Moderate Risk Behaviors," *Journal of Infectious Diseases* 180:65 (November 1999): 1624-1631.

116 "New Research Shows Dangers of Condoms in HIV Prevention," *Culture & Cosmos* 1:23 (13 January 2004). (Emphasis mine).

117 Centers for Disease Control and Prevention Press Release, January 13, 2009 (available at www.cdc.gov).

118 Haishan Fu, et al., "Contraceptive Failure Rates: New Estimates From the 1995 National Survey of Family Growth," *Family Planning Perspectives* 31:2 (March/April, 1999): 60.

119 Haishan Fu, et al., 61.

120 Santelli, et al., "Contraceptive Use and Pregnancy Risk Among U.S. High School Students, 1991-2003," *Perspectives on Sexual and Reproductive Health* 38:2 (June, 2006): 109.

121 Cf. Yovel, et al., "The Effects of Sex, Menstrual Cycle, and Oral Contraceptives on the Number and Activity of Natural Killer Cells," *Gynecologic Oncology* 81:2 (May, 2001): 254-262; Blum, et al., "Antisperm Antibodies in Young Oral Contraceptive Users," *Advances in Contraception* 5 (1989): 41-46; Critchlow, et al., "Determinants of Cervical Ectopia and of Cervicitis: Age, Oral Contraception, Specific Cervical Infection, Smoking, and Douching," *American Journal of Obstetrics and Gynecology* 173:2 (August, 1995): 534-43.

122 Cf. Baeten, et al., Hormonal Contraception and Risk of Sexually Transmitted Disease Acquisition: Results from a Prospective Study," *American Journal of Obstetrics and Gynecology* 185:2 (August, 2001): 380-385; Ley, et al., "Determinants of Genital Human Papillomavirus Infection in Young Women," *Journal of the National Cancer Institute* 83:14 (July, 1991): 997-1003; Prakash, et al., "Oral Contraceptive Use Induces Upregulation of the CCR5 Chemokine Receptor on CD4(+) T cells in the Cervical Epithelium of Healthy Women," *Journal of Reproductive Immunology* 54 (March, 2002): 117-131; Wang, et al., "Risk of HIV Infection in Oral Contraceptive Pill Users: A Meta-Analysis," *Journal of Acquired Immune Deficiency Syndromes* 21:1 (May, 1999): 51-58; Lavreys, et al., "Hormonal Contraception and Risk of HIV-1 Acquisition: Results from a 10-year Prospective Study," *AIDS* 18:4 (March, 2004): 695-697.

123 Cf. Chris Kahlenborn, MD, et al., "Oral Contraceptive Use as a Risk Factor for Premenopausal Breast Cancer: A Meta-analysis," *Mayo Clinic Proceedings* 81:10 (October, 2006): 1290-1302; Collaborative Group on Hormonal Factors in Breast Cancer, "Breast Cancer and hormonal contraceptives: collaborative reanalysis of individual data on 53,297 Women with Breast Cancer and 100,239 Women without Breast Cancer from 54 Epidemiological Studies," *Lancet* 347 (June, 1996):

1713-1727; World Health Organization, "IARC Monographs Programme Finds Combined Estrogen-Progestogen Contraceptives and Menopausal Therapy are Carcinogenic to Humans," International Agency for Research on Cancer, Press Release 167 (July 29, 2005).

124   Cf. Smith, et al., "Cervical Aancer and Use of Hormonal Contraceptives: A Systematic Review," *Lancet* 361 (2003): 1159-1167.

125   Cf. World Health Organization, "IARC Monographs Programme Finds Combined Estrogen-Progestogen Contraceptives and Menopausal Therapy are Carcinogenic to Humans," International Agency for Research on Cancer, Press Release 167 (July 29, 2005); La Vecchia, "Oral contraceptives and cancer," *Minerva Ginecologica* 58:3 (June, 2006): 209-214.

126   Cf. *Physicians' Desk Reference*, 2415; Kemmeren, et al., "Third Generation Oral Contraceptives and Risk of Venous Thrombosis: Meta Analysis," *British Medical Journal* 323 (July, 2001): 131-134; Parkin, et al., "Oral Contraceptives and Fatal Pulmonary Embolism," *The Lancet* 355:9221 (June, 2000): 2133-2134; Hedenmalm, et al., "Fatal Venous Thromboembolism Associated with Different Combined Oral Contraceptives," *Drug Safety* 28:10 (2005): 907-916; Sameuelsson, et al., "Mortality from Venous Thromboembolism in Young Swedish Women and its Relation to Pregnancy and Use of Oral Contraceptives," *European Journal of Epidemiology* 20:6 (2005): 509-516.

127   Cf. *Physicians' Desk Reference*, (Montvale, N.J.: Thomson, 2006), 2414; Julia Warnock, et al., "Comparison of Androgens in Women with Hypoactive Sexual Desire Disorder: Those on Combined Oral Contraceptives (COCs) vs. Those not on COCs," *The Journal of Sexual Medicine* 3:5 (September 2006): 878-882; Cf. Panzer, et al., "Impact of Oral Contraceptives on Sex Hormone-Binding Globulin and Androgen Levels: A Retrospective Study in Women with Sexual Dysfunction," *Journal of Sexual Medicine* 3:1 (January 2006): 104-113; "Can Taking the Pill Dull a Woman's Desire Forever?" *New Scientist* (27 May 2005), 17.

128   T.A. Kiersch, "Treatment of Sex Offenders with Depo-Provera," *The Bulletin of the American Academy of Psychiatry and the Law* 18:2 (1990): 179-187; California Penal Code Section 645.

129   "The Case Against Depo-Provera: Problems in the U.S.," *Multinational Monitor* 6:2-3 (February/March, 1985); Depo-Provera, Patient Labeling, Pharmacia & Upjohn Company (October 2004).

130   Robert Rector, "Facts about Abstinence Education," The Heritage Foundation (30 March 2004).

131   Blesseds in the Year 2005 "Anacleto González Flores and 8 Companions," www.vatican.va

132   Victoria J. Rideout M.A., Ulla G. Foehr, M.A., and Donald F. Roberts, Ph. D., "Generation M2: Media in the Lives of 8- to 18-Year-olds," A Kaiser Family Foundation Study, January 2010.

133   Cope-Farrar KM, Kunkel D., "Sexual Messages in Teens' Favorite Prime-Time Television Programs," In: Brown JD, Steele JR, Walsh-Childers K, eds. *Sexual Teens, Sexual Media: Investigating Media's Influence on Adolescent Sexuality* (Mahwah, NJ: Lawrence Erlbaum, 2002), 59-78.

134 Kunkel, et al., "Sex on TV 4," A Kaiser Family Foundation Study (November 2005), 38.

135 Jane Brown, et al., "Sexy Media Matter: Exposure to Sexual Content in Music, Movies, Television, and Magazines Predicts Black and White Adolescents' Sexual Behavior," *Pediatrics* 117:4 (April 2006): 1018-1027; Anita Chandra, et al., "Does Watching Sex on Television Predict Teen Pregnancy? Findings From a National Longitudinal Survey of Youth," *Pediatrics* 122:5 (November 2008): 1047-1054.

136 RAND Corporation Research Highlights: "Does Watching Sex on Television influence Teens' Sexual Activity?" *Pediatrics* 114:3 (September 2004); cf. Collins, et al., "Entertainment Television as a Healthy Sex Educator: The Impact of Condom-Efficacy Information in an Episode of *Friends*," *Pediatrics,* 112:5 (November 2003): 1115-1121.

137 Victoria J. Rideout M.A., Ulla G. Foehr, M.A., and Donald F. Roberts, Ph. D., "Generation M2: Media in the Lives of 8- to 18-Year-olds," A Kaiser Family Foundation Study, January 2010.

138 Victoria J. Rideout M.A., Ulla G. Foehr, M.A., and Donald F. Roberts, Ph. D., "Generation M2: Media in the Lives of 8- to 18-Year-olds," A Kaiser Family Foundation Study, January 2010.

139 Victoria J. Rideout M.A., Ulla G. Foehr, M.A., and Donald F. Roberts, Ph. D., "Generation M2: Media in the Lives of 8- to 18-Year-olds," A Kaiser Family Foundation Study, January 2010.

140 Victoria J. Rideout M.A., Ulla G. Foehr, M.A., and Donald F. Roberts, Ph. D., "Generation M2: Media in the Lives of 8- to 18-Year-olds," A Kaiser Family Foundation Study, January 2010.

141 Victoria J. Rideout M.A., Ulla G. Foehr, M.A., and Donald F. Roberts, Ph. D., "Generation M2: Media in the Lives of 8- to 18-Year-olds," A Kaiser Family Foundation Study, January 2010.

142 Internet Pornography Statistics, Jerry Ropelato, http://www.Internet-filter-review. toptenreviews.com/Internet-pornography-statistics.html

143 Internet Pornography Statistics, Jerry Ropelato, http://www.Internet-filter-review. toptenreviews.com/Internet-pornography-statistics.html

144 Internet Pornography Statistics, Jerry Ropelato, http://www.Internet-filter-review. toptenreviews.com/Internet-pornography-statistics.html

145 Victoria J. Rideout M.A., Ulla G. Foehr, M.A., and Donald F. Roberts, Ph. D., "Generation M2: Media in the Lives of 8- to 18-Year-olds," A Kaiser Family Foundation Study, January 2010.

146 Victoria J. Rideout M.A., Ulla G. Foehr, M.A., and Donald F. Roberts, Ph. D., "Generation M2: Media in the Lives of 8- to 18-Year-olds," A Kaiser Family Foundation Study, January 2010.

147 "Sex and Tech," Results from a Survey of Teens and Young Adults, National Campaign to Prevent Teen Pregnancy (2009), 1.

148 Victoria J. Rideout M.A., Ulla G. Foehr, M.A., and Donald F. Roberts, Ph. D., "Generation M2: Media in the Lives of 8- to 18-Year-olds," A Kaiser Family Foundation Study, January 2010.

149 St. Gianna Molla, *Love is a Choice: The Life of St. Gianna Molla*, Ignatius Press (DVD).

150 B.C. Miller, et al., "Dating Age and Stage as Correlates of Adolescent Sexual Attitudes and Behavior," *Journal of Adolescent Research* 1:3 (1986): 367.

151 Pope John Paul II, address, April 29, 1989, Antananarivo, Madagascar. As quoted by Pedro Beteta López, ed., *The Meaning of Vocation* (Princeton, N.J.: Scepter Publishers, 1997), 28.

152 Suzanne Ryan, et al., "The First Time: Characteristics of Teens' First Sexual Relationships," *Research Brief* (Washington, D.C.: Child Trends, August 2003), 2.

153 Hsu G., "Statutory Rape: The Dirty Secret Behind Teen Sex Numbers," *Family Policy* (1996): 1-16.

154 Trudee Tarkowski, et al., "Epidemiology of Human Papillomavirus Infection and Abnormal Cytologic Test Results in an Urban Adolescent Population," *Journal of Infectious Diseases* 189 (1 January 2004): 49.

155 The National Center on Addiction and Substance Abuse, "National Survey of American Attitudes on Substance Abuse IX: Teen Dating Practices and Sexual Activity," Columbia University (August 2004), 6.

156 *The Truth and Meaning of Human Sexuality*, 133.

157 *The Truth and Meaning of Human Sexuality*, 65.

158 *The Truth and Meaning of Human Sexuality*, 129-132.

159 *The Truth and Meaning of Human Sexuality*, 124.2

160 J. Jaccard, et al., "Parent-Adolescent Congruency in Reports of Adolescent Sexual Behavior and in Communications About Sexual Behavior," *Child Development* 69:1 (February 1998): 247-261.

161 *The Truth and Meaning of Human Sexuality*, 78.

162 *The Truth and Meaning of Human Sexuality*, 83.

163 *The Truth and Meaning of Human Sexuality*, 76.

164 *God's Design for Sex* (Series), by Brenna B. Jones and Carolyn Nystrom; *Angel in the Waters*, by Regina Doman and Ben Hatke; *The Joyful Mysteries of Life*, by Catherine and Bernard Scherrer; *You are a Masterpiece* (DVD); *The Preborn Christ*, by Susan Brindle, *The Princess and the Kiss* and *The Squire And The Scroll* by Jennie Bishop.

165 Walter Mischel and Yuichi Shoda, "The Nature of Adolescent Competencies Predicted by Preschool Delay of Gratification," *Journal of Personality and Social Psychology* 54:4 (1988): 687-696; Mischel, et al., "Delay of Gratification in Children," *Science* 244:4907 (26 May 1989): 933-938; Shoda and Mischel, "Predicting Adolescent Cognitive and Self-Regulatory Competencies From Preschool Delay of Gratification: Identifying Diagnostic Conditions," *Developmental Psychology* 26:6 (1990): 978-986.

166 *The Truth and Meaning of Human Sexuality*, 82.

167 *The Truth and Meaning of Human Sexuality*, 104.

168 Katy Perry, "I Kissed a Girl," Capitol Records.

169 *The Truth and Meaning of Human Sexuality*, 88, 89.

170 *The Truth and Meaning of Human Sexuality*, 93.

171 *Catechism of the Catholic Church*, 2352.

172 *The Truth and Meaning of Human Sexuality*, 103.

173 *The Truth and Meaning of Human Sexuality*, 16.

174   Cf. Jason Evert, *If You Really Loved Me: 100 Questions on Dating, Relationships, and Sexual Purity* (El Cajon, CA.: Catholic Answers, 2009).

175   *The Truth and Meaning of Human Sexuality*, 67.

176   *The Truth and Meaning of Human Sexuality*, 126.3, 127.4

177   *The Truth and Meaning of Human Sexuality*, 122.1

178   *Gaudium et Spes*, 24.

179   "With One Voice 2002: America's Adults and Teens Sound Off About Teen Pregnancy," The National Campaign to Prevent Teen Pregnancy, (December 2002).

180   Whitaker D.J., Miller K.S., "Parent-Adolescent Discussions about Sex and Condoms: Impact on Peer Influences of Sexual Risk Behavior," *Journal of Adolescent Research* 15:2 (2000): 251-273.

181   *The Truth and Meaning of Human Sexuality*, 91.

182   Cf. P. Frank-Herrmann, et al., "The Effectiveness of a Fertility Awareness Based Method to Avoid Pregnancy in Relation to a Couple's Sexual Behaviour During the Fertile Time: A Prospective Longitudinal Study," *Human Reproduction* (February 2007): 1-10; R. E. J. Ryder, "'Natural Family Planning': Effective Birth Control Supported by the Catholic Church," *British Medical Journal* 307 (1993): 723-726.

183   Cf. Irit Sinai and Marcos Arévalo, "It's All in the Timing: Coital Frequency and Fertility Awareness-Based Methods of Family Planning," *Journal of Biosocial Science* 38:6 (November 2006): 763-777.

184   Charlotte Hays, "Solving the Puzzle of Natural Family Planning," *Crisis* (December 2001): 15.

185   *Faithful to Each Other For Ever: A Catholic Handbook of Pastoral Help for Marriage Preparation* (Washington D.C.: United States Catholic Conference, 1989), 46.

186   *Humanae Vitae*, 21.

187   J. Budziszewski, in Sam and Bethany Torode, *Open Embrace* (Grand Rapids, Mich.: Eerdmans, 2002), xvi.

188   National Prayer Breakfast, sponsored by the U.S. Senate and House of Representatives (3 February 1994).

189   *The Truth and Meaning of Human Sexuality*, 19-21.

190   Pope John Paul II, *Gift and Mystery*, 20.

191   *The Truth and Meaning of Human Sexuality*, 27.

192   *Familiaris Consortio*, 39.

Jason Evert holds a master's degree in theology and undergraduate degrees in counseling and theology from Franciscan University of Steubenville. He is the author of more than 10 books, including *If You Really Loved Me*, and *How to Find Your Soulmate without Losing Your Soul*, which challenge young people to embrace the virtue of chastity. Each year, Jason speaks to more than 100,000 teens in high schools and colleges internationally.

Speaker and author, Chris Stefanick, is director of Youth, Young Adult and Campus Ministry for the Archdiocese of Denver. He lives in Colorado with his wife Natalie and their five children: Rosemary, Ethan, Genevieve, Joseph and Eloise.

BRING THESE POWERFUL DISPLAYS TO YOUR CHURCH,
SCHOOL, BUSINESS OR RETREAT CENTER, AND GIVE
OTHERS THE CHANCE TO OBTAIN CHASTITY RESOURCES
AND OTHER INSPIRATIONAL PRODUCTS BY VISITING

CHASTITYPROJECT.COM

THE SEXUAL CULTURE WAR IS ON

SEXTING, FACEBOOK GOSSIP, PORNOGRAPHY, HOOKING UP, BROKEN FAMILIES, AND BROKEN HEARTS.

HOW DO YOU TURN PEER PRESSURE INTO PURE PRESSURE?

Jason and Crystalina Evert have spoken to more than one million teens on five continents. Now, schedule a presentation to have them inspire the youth in your junior high, high school, university, church, or conference.

Teens today need straight answers to tough questions about dating, relationships, and sexual purity. That's why Chastity Project offers more than a dozen presentations designed to empower students and parents.

FOR MORE INFORMATION, VISIT

CHASTITY PROJECT.COM

FOR $2 OR LESS, WHO WOULD YOU GIVE THESE BOOKS AND CDS TO?

In order to reach as many people as possible, more than 20 chastity CDs and books (including the one you're reading) are available in bulk orders for $2 or less! Therefore, share this book and others like it with the people in your life who need it right now. For example:

YOUR COLLEGE DORM

YOUR HIGH SCHOOL

YOUR YOUTH OR YOUNG ADULT GROUP AT CHURCH

YOUR ALMA MATER

Buy a case of books and donate them as gifts at graduation, freshman orientation, retreats, conferences, confirmation, as a missionary effort through campus ministry, or to people you meet anywhere. You never know whose life you could change.

TO ORDER, VISIT